Sustainable Finance

Series Editors

Sustainable Finance is a concise and authoritative reference series linking research and practice. It provides reliable concepts and research findings in the ever growing field of sustainable investing and finance, SDG economics and Leadership with the declared commitment to present the theories, methods, tools and investment approaches that can fulfil the United Nations Sustainable Development Goals and the Paris Agreement COP 21/22 alongside with de-risking assets and creating triple purpose solutions that ensure the parity of profit, people and planet through choice architecture passion and performance. The series addresses market failure, systemic risk and reinvents portfolio theory, portfolio engineering as well as behavioural finance, financial mediation, product innovation, shared values, community building, business strategy and innovation, exponential tech and creation of social capital. Sustainable Finance and SDG Economics series helps to understand keynotes on international guidelines, guiding accounting and accountability principles, prototyping new developments in triple bottom line investing, cost benefit analysis, integrated financial first plus impact first concepts and impact measurement. Going beyond adjacent fields (like accounting, marketing, strategy, risk management) it integrates the concept of psychology, innovation, exponential tech, choice architecture, alternative economics, blue economy shared values, professions of the future, leadership, human and community development, team culture, impact, quantitative and qualitative measurement, Harvard Negotiation, mediation and complementary currency design using exponential tech and ledger technology. Books in the series contain latest findings from research, concepts for implementation, as well as best practices and case studies for the finance industry.

Karen Wendt

Social Stock Exchanges

Catalyst for Impact Investing?

Springer

Karen Wendt
Sustainable Finance C/O
Eccos Impact GmbH
Cham, Switzerland

ISSN 2522-8285 ISSN 2522-8293 (electronic)
Sustainable Finance
ISBN 978-3-030-99719-9 ISBN 978-3-030-99720-5 (eBook)
https://doi.org/10.1007/978-3-030-99720-5

This Springer imprint is published by the registered company Springer Nature Switzerland AG
The registered company address is: Gewerbestrasse 11, 6330 Cham, Switzerland

About the Book

This research researches the role of stock exchanges in catalysing impact investing. Stock exchanges are marketplaces providing liquidity, marketability and pricing to securitized assets. Through the process of disinvestment and reinvestment, savings will turn into investment avenues. This leads to capital formation and economic growth. Existing legal framework provides a safe and fair deal in security markets. The question of using stock exchanges as listing platforms for assets that intentionally create a positive impact for society providing the securitized enterprises with alternative fundraising structures, Social Stock Exchanges (SSEs) is relevant if one wishes to redirect capital to sustainable growth (see 2. . . .). The combination of a special listing procedure combined with increased marketability could provide the so-called Impact or Social Stocks with additional liquidity, growth opportunities and marketability, create necessary transparency through listing criteria and market making and could harmonize scattered private markets where only alternative asset owners can invest and provide a clear distinction between ESG (risk management-oriented approaches) and impact investing. The UK, Canada, Singapore, South Africa and Brazil have l SSEs, India and Switzerland and other countries are in the process of creating them. On the regulatory front, The European Union has issued its Action Plan for Sustainable Growth with the declared goal to redirect capital to Sustainable Growth including a green taxonomy, a forthcoming social and brown taxonomy. Based on interviews with Members of the EU High Level Group, this research discovers, documents, evaluates and categorizes how and in what ways entrepreneurs solve environmental or social problems using market mechanisms and methodologies, creating ecosocial and economic/financial performance at the same time. The author analyses how impact investing can be differentiated from environmental and social governance (ESG) and provides an overview of what Social Stock Exchanges do well already, what can be improved and how SSEs will impact the redirection of capital in the financial market. The terms Impact Stock Exchanges (ISEs) and Social Stock Exchanges (SSEs) will be used in an interchangeable manner. In the evaluation of what stock exchanges provide, the author will use the emerging taxonomies around the world, the seven capitals model developed by Flora and Flora (2011) used in multinational institutions like the International Finance Corporation (IFC) and Barile viable systems approach to analyse their prospects. This will include the concepts of green bonds, social bonds and social entrepreneurship finance on stock exchanges. This contribution is developed on the basis of frameworks and systems approaches which are intended as a theoretical framework for the analysis of social phenomena as well as for orienting decision making. The author will systemize and analyse how these concepts dovetail to the concepts of existing stock markets and make proposals on what needs to be improved to make SSEs successful.

One question is whether impact assets will further need special platforms for impact transactions—known as Social Stock Exchanges or whether they progress in a way that they are compatible with existing market structures and can be placed on traditional marketplaces like bond markets and stock markets. Also, the author is spotting for which assets structures this is the case and where this is not the case and so differentiate between the market maturity and design of impact assets regarding their compatibility with existing traditional markets and—if not compatible whether social stock exchanges will provide a solution.

Contents

1 Introductions 1
1.1 Research Design 5

2 Literature Review 7
2.1 Concepts of Sustainability 7
Viable Systems Model 8
2.2 The Emerging Role of Taxonomies 11
The EU Action Plan for Sustainable Growth and the EU Taxonomy 12
Asian Taxonomies: China, Malaysia, Singapore and others 15
2.3 Impact Investing Versus ESG Approaches 17
2.4 The Perceived Need of Impact Stock Exchanges or Social Stock Exchanges 21
2.5 The Current State of SSEs and ISEs 23
2.6 Review of Scientific Literature And Practitioners' View on SSEs 26
Mapping the Functions of SSEs 27
Practitioners' View on Social Stock Exchanges/Impact Stock Exchanges 27
Academic View on Social Stock Exchanges/Impact Stock Exchanges 30
2.7 Impact Investing 32
Addressing the Inconsistencies of Impact Investing 32
Definitions of Impact Investing 34
2.8 Assessing Impact Investment Practices: Tools, Frameworks and Databases 36
2.9 Conclusions on Impact Investing and Its Problematic for Stock Exchanges 39
2.10 Existing Product Structures with Impact Used at SSEs or in the Traditional Stock and Bonds Markets 41
2.11 Social Entrepreneurship and Social Economy Finance 43

2.12 Green Bonds 52
Conclusions and Learning When Contrasting Green Bonds to Impact Assets 54
2.13 Social Impact Bonds 57

3 Traditional Stock Exchanges 61
3.1 Functions of Stock Exchanges 61
3.2 Comparing Traditional Markets Key Determinants with the SSEs 62
3.3 Blueprinting Social Stock Exchanges 63
3.4 Social Stock Exchanges and Their Challenges 71

4 Critical analysis and Prognosis on the Development of SSEs 77
4.1 Prognosis on the Development of SSEs 77
4.2 Recommendations for an Ecosystems Approach of SSEs 79
4.3 Outlook 81

5 Conclusions and Limitations 83

References 87

Chapter 1
Introductions

Social Stock Exchanges are a new socio-economic phenomenon. Attracting investment seems to be one of the main problems of social and ecological oriented entrepreneurs. SSEs are trading and exchange platforms that allow social and green businesses to raise capital by attracting investors willing to invest in businesses that create blended value and apply a lockstep approach. They address the need for a dedicated liquid marketplace with transparent price building mechanisms. As benefits of social stock exchanges the following have been raised by practitioners and researchers (see Chap. 2).

According to existing SSEs Social enterprises are a new operating model addressing acute societal and environmental challenges that have gained a global consensus through the UN SDGs (United Nations, 2017). While the impact investment market is growing at an average annual rate of 20%, hurdles still prevent it from becoming mainstream, including, the creation, sourcing and evaluation of investment opportunities, transaction sizes, viable exit options, and impact measurement (SwissOX, 2021).

Calandra and Favareto (2020), Boguslavskaya and Demushkina (2013), Pavlov (2017, 2019), Wendt (2017) found that SSEs make the procedure of impact investment easier; increase the transparency of ecosocial projects; save transaction costs; provide immediate liquidity to ecosocial enterprises; provide transparent information and therefore allow for a fair valuation process, the placement on the exchange alone increases the ecosocial value and often the valuation of investments and the idea is to enable investors to harvest a financial and an eco-social return on investment. This claim will be reviewed here.

K. Wendt, *Social Stock Exchanges*, Sustainable Finance,
https://doi.org/10.1007/978-3-030-99720-5_1

Many funds, institutional investors and asset managers would like to go into impact investments. However, they appear to be "hindered" by the system. This publication therefore aims to find out what prevents Institutional Investors from investing in impact investments and how the market could be stimulated.

Some of the questions we like to address in the interviews are:

1. How great is the appetite of Institutional Investors for impact investments?
2. Is there a market failure and from where / by what does it arise?
3. Could Impact Stock Exchanges (ISEs) or a special impact segment at a regulated stock exchange mediate / eliminate this market failure?
4. Do ISE in their current form fit the market? How should a re- design of ISEs look like? How should a special segment for impact investment at a regulated stock exchange look like?

SSEs have been born in business and there is little research on their impact on redirecting capital to sustainable purposes. With the large and growing market of medium-sized green-tech, green energy and social enterprises globally and their significant lack of access to financing, coupled with a growing investors' demand for impact investments, it is relevant to understand the contribution that SSEs provide in redirecting capital to eco-social impact investments, where they succeed and where they fail. This may lead to a couple of suggestions what needs to be improve.

Since the 2007/2008 financial crisis, many questions have been posed about how financial markets operate and how they are able to benefit society (Shiller, 2013; Zingales, 2015). The contribution made by financial markets and financial institutions to the prosperity of society has been questioned and the need to develop new investment opportunities able to create blended return and shared value have emerged (Kramer & Porter, 2011; Lehner, 2016a, 2016b; Weber & Feltmate, 2016a, 2016b; Jacobs & Mazzucato, 2016). Around the globe, new investment models able to reflect responsible behaviour have been claimed in order to keep financial markets in tune with the development of society.

Investing with the joint purpose of financial return and a desired social or environmental impact is on the rise according to the Global Impact Investing Network GIIN (GIIN (2016b)), with market size estimates of up to USD 1 trillion by 2020 according to O'Donohoe et al. (2010). However, there is not yet a segment on stock exchanges of impact investments or social enterprises according to Kleissner—the founder of the GIN network (Kleissner (2018)). Today impact investing is mostly the domain of wealthy individuals, foundations, and family offices. Non-accredited investors and/or retail investors plus pensions funds are not yet able to meaningfully participate in this new way of investing (Kleissner (2018)).

At the same time the following megatrends can be identified:

1. The recent upsurge in entrepreneurship in many countries (Fairlie et al. (2015); OECD (2016); Schawbel (2017)),
2. shifting attitudes towards the role of business in society (Deloitte, 2016), and
3. a broad policy push for sustainable development which materialized in the 17 Sustainable Development Goals (SDG) and the Paris Agreement (UN, 2015; UNFCCC, 2015).

However, a more recent survey by Barclays (2017) found that despite the widespread interest in the topic, very few investors have actually made impact investments. Practitioners in the field often emphasize a chronic lack of investment-ready projects like the "Finanazagentur for Social Entrepreneurship "FASE and the Global Impact Investing Network GIIN (FASE (2016); GIIN (2016a). This might be an effect caused by limited market access or high transaction costs. Although considerable networking efforts have been made to boost investor demand and establish the necessary infrastructure (see e.g. WEF 2013; Schwartz et al., 2015; Rexhepi, 2016), thus far, impact investing has remained the domain of relatively few wealthy individuals, family offices and foundations, while non-accredited investors and pension funds cannot participate in this newly emerged market (Kleissner 2018). According to Kleissner investees lack access to products available to more affluent investors, and a lack of transaction platforms (ibid). It has been argued that not enough assets can be found that match the impact definition (ibid). The creation of regulated funding platforms known as social stock or impact exchanges (SSEs) has been proposed by practitioners as a necessary step towards democratizing and popularizing impact investing, easing the asset search process for investors and capital access for entrepreneurs. While the need for SSE is heavily debated in expert circles along with the challenges they may bring about, the first SSEs have come into existence in the UK, US, Canada, and Singapore, complemented by some smaller SSEs in Brazil, South Africa and Kenya.

Social stock or impact exchanges (referred to as SSEs) have been proposed as a key step in achieving the objective of attracting capital and investors (Nicholls & Patton, 2015, p. 324). Lehner and Nicholls recommend to combine elements of existing crowd-funding (see Lehner & Nicholls, 2014), peer-to-peer lending, philanthropic loan or donation, and other comparable platforms. An interesting question is whether fully fledged and regulated SSEs would essentially operate just like conventional stock exchanges by serving as "market places for listing, trading, settlement and clearance of shares, bonds, and other financial instruments issued by or for social and green businesses, albeit in the context of highly specific listing and reporting requirements" (Shahnaz et al. (2014, p. 157)).

Since the economic crisis triggered in 2008 the concept of impact investing emerged. Impact Investing has initially been a term coined by the Rockefeller Foundation. Impact creation was necessary "because governments, charities, philanthropists alone were no longer capable of dealing with the twenty-first century's social and environmental challenges. Focussing on the act of charitable giving rather than on achieving social outcomes and a dependence on unpredictable funding hindered many charitable organizations from realizing their full potential concerning innovations, effectiveness and scale" (Brandstetter & Lehner, 2015). The World Economic Forum recently acknowledged the role the investment and finance sector can play in creating solutions to social problems and stated: "Given the nature of how resources are distributed in the world, private investors may have a special role and responsibility in addressing social challenges." (World Economic Forum 2013). Yet apart from a small number of specialized forms of impact investing like social impact bonds, green bonds and mission related philanthropic investments little is known about the complex interplay between entrepreneurs or organizations, intermediaries, investor regulations and the successful use of instruments in the field. Glänzel & Scheuerle (2016) use the term social impact investing to clearly distinguish from finance first approaches of impact investing that have a stronger commercial orientation. Hummels & de Leede (2014) enclose impact investing in the wider category of responsible investing, of which is only a part while Hebb (2013), Pretorius & Giamporcaro (2012), Viviers & Firer (2013) and Viviers et al. (2011) considers impact investing as 'responsible investing'. Shulman and George (2012) consider impact investing as a form of Socially Responsible Investing (SRI) while Geobey and Weber (2013) clarify that SRI screen out investments for social, environmental or governance reasons while impact investing is based on the assumption that investments can create financial returns and address social and environmental challenges simultaneously. Impact investing is also included by many authors in the social finance landscape (Suetin, 2011; Geobey & Weber, 2013; Geobey et al., 2012; Mendell & Barbosa, 2013; Weber, 2013; Weber, 2016a, 2016b).

In the following chapters some critical positionings about the definition of sustaibability, impact investing and the creation and financing process of eco-social solutions and products with market mechanisms and the role of different conceptualisations of capital are provided. The author will also examine and map the promises of Social Stock Exchanges, or Impact Stock Exchanges (SSEs and ISEs used interchangeably) and analyse how far impact assets in the definition of the EU Action Plan have progressed into financial markets. One question is whether they will further need special platforms for impact transactions -known as Social Stock Exchanges or whether they progress in a way that they are compatible with existing market places like bond markets and stock markets. Also the author is spotting where this is the case and where this is not the case and so differentiate between the market maturity and design of impact assets. This research is unique in that it investigates if and in what way SSEs might catalyse redirecting capital to sustainable growth and analyses success stories and short comings. This task requires a systems perspective in order to depict the dynamics and cause- effects relationships. It is the first one to analyse the impact of SSEs using the tools of policy making and market intervention appraisal. Therefore the work aims to contribute to the emerging field of literature n SSEs, the business models that exist and tools that catalyse the money flow to eco-social impact enterprises.

The rest of the book organised as followed. The next chapter will assess an in-depth literature review the role of taxonomies, impact investing, and ISEs/SSEs in their current form, the state of impact investing and the impact of the new emerging taxonomies on impact investing and stock exchange. It will also provide an analysis of products and how well they managed to enter the stock market. Chap. 3 analyses the current market structure and how well the products dovetails of the market mechanisms existing at stock exchanges. Chap. 4 will provide a critical analysis of the shortcomings and make proposals on how to address the market better –.

1.1 Research Design

In the following, the methodological approach of this study is characterized.

The goal of this work is the creation of a methodology for ISEs/SSEs and thus the theory building. Therefore, a less structured approach is deliberately chosen, which allows for unexpected findings.

The relevant data will be gathered by means of literature study. With the primary goal of gaining a new methodology and associated new insights in the young research field of ISEs/SSEs, this study is located in the area of basic research. Developing a ISE/SSE blueprinting methodology based on dimensions and indicators, which allows a transparent and scientifically-based assessment of impact investments appears an obvious necessity. In addition, removing obstacles that block Institutional Investors from investing can catalyse and scale the impact investing market in a harmonized manner.

Research and Assessment on SSEs has been rudimentary and in its infancy, an explorative research design therefore is used. Results of the pre-study (Wendt 2020) indicate that it is difficult for institutional investors to invest in impact due to various factors such as lot sizes, fiduciary duties, liquidity and fungibility of assets and also due to the lack of market making and lack of blueprinting. Therefore, a hypothesis-generating qualitative literature driven methodology is employed. The resulting conclusions and recommendations are directly anchored in the collected data.

One of the Research Focus is the thus far under-researched Institutional Investors segment and how they can be matched effectively and efficiently with the under-researched alternative asset classes in social entrepreneurship. With the green bond, the social impact bond and the project finance infrastructure bonds there are already three products that are compatible with for the financial markets. Nevertheless the author is referring to them where appropriate in order to gain understanding on how the undercapitalized structures in impact investing could profit from this knowledge.

Chapter 2
Literature Review

2.1 Concepts of Sustainability

According to Barile et al. (2018) sustainability has been shaped by corporate social responsibility. In a traditional view stemming from the Corporate Social Responsibility World the inevitable consequence of wanting to compress sustainability operational rules in an ideal direction has resulted in the definition of three dimensions that specify sustainability (description according to Barile et al. (2018)):

Economic sustainability, as the ability to efficiently use the available resources to assure economic growth.

Social sustainability, as the ability to ensure conditions of stability, democracy, participation, respect for human rights and international labour laws, equal access to education and justice, as well as the possibility to guarantee that human welfare conditions (safety, health) are equally distributed among classes and genders. These requests were found first in a compulsory manner in Prof. Ruggies Protect, Respect, Remedy Framework which he produced as an advisor to the UN (Ruggie, 2011).

Environmental sustainability, as the ability to maintain the quality and the reproducibility of the natural resources. This requirement was first found by Carlowitz (1680) in his use only what you can reproduce approach.

The idea of the triple bottom line was first expressed by John Elkington him famous book Partnership from Cannibals with Forks. It was Elkington himself you admitted in a rewrite this year that the triple bottom line needs overhauls and a shift to a new paradigm, as it was reductionist anddoesnt depict the interplay between these three dimensions (Elkington, 2021).

In order to understand the synergies, interplay and dynamics between the dimensions we need to understand how the synergetic energy flow among these dimensions—which can be either positive or negative—resulting in the growth or diminishment of these dimensions. According to Barile et al. (2018) the intersection between the considered dimensions determines the conditions of development that can be defined as viable (environment and economic), equitable (social and

K. Wendt, *Social Stock Exchanges*, Sustainable Finance,
https://doi.org/10.1007/978-3-030-99720-5_2

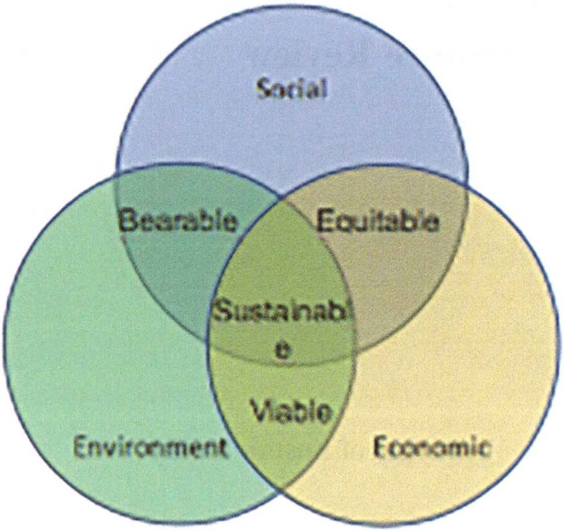

Fig. 2.1 Own representation drawing from Barile et al. (2018)

economic), and bearable (environment and social). According to Barile et al. (2018) drawing from system theory and the viable systems organisation model posit that "These dimensions appear to be preliminary, but are also necessary and sufficient for a full implementation of a commonly shared approach to sustainability. The interplay between these three dimensions is depicted in Fig. 2.1.

Viable Systems Model

With this interpretation Barile et al. (2018) provide a more dynamic approach to sustainability, as they take an integrated dynamic look at the three dimensions and do not treat them as separate pillars. Thereby they allow to analyse the interplay and the process how the desired intersection of the three dimension can be achieved, constructed and maximised.

Jaeggi et al. (2018) seek to provide frameworks that help understand better how sustainable finance can be disseminated both within and beyond the financial sector. There are two fundamentally different understandings of "sustainable": first, the long-standing notion of long-term stability financial or political including extra-financial risks from the environmental and social sphere and, second, the more modern use in the context of sustainable resource use and sustainable development (Jaeggi et al. 2018). The second definition is more pro-active and future oriented as its ambition is to shape the world through sustainable development an expression stemming from development finance organisations Jaeggi et al. (2018). It is

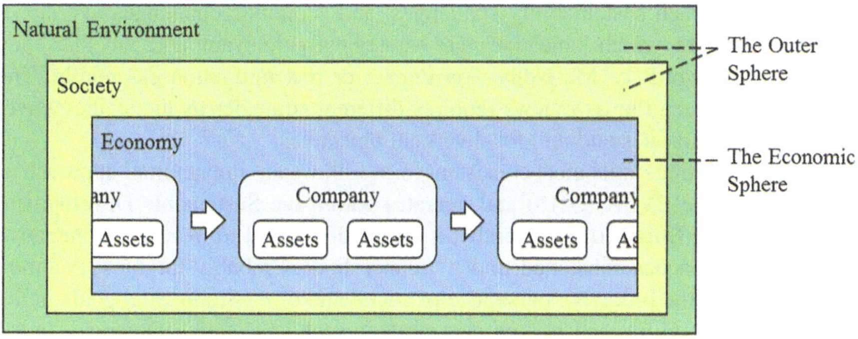

Fig. 2.2 Own representation based on Jaeggi et al. (2018)

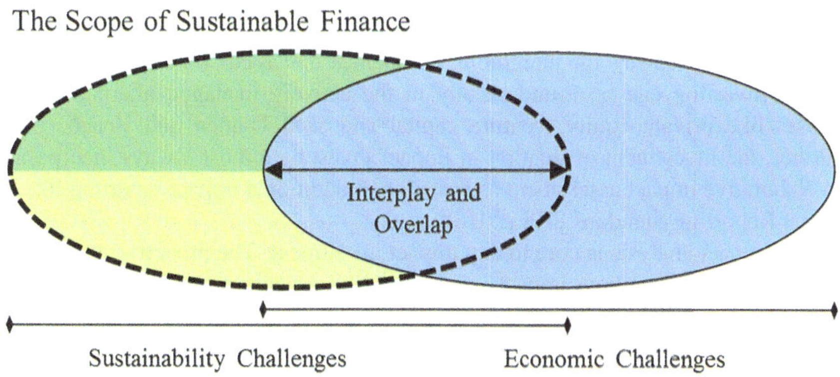

Fig. 2.3 Interplay between economic and sustainability challenges

important to differentiate between the two views, as they cover largely different issues, might aim for divergent objectives, and require different strategies.

The economic sphere is described as containing companies and the assets that they own, whereas society and natural environment are treated as externalities (Fig. 2.2).

Whereas the traditional definition of sustainability sees the environment as an externality (and consequently includes it into the sphere of market failure), the emerging definition is looking into the system dynamics and overlap between financial and eco-social issues and return. When discussing sustainability in the traditional model, the discussions primarily focus on the outer sphere, and on how the sustainability challenges that are observed in the outer sphere might affect or be affected by the economic sphere and the entities it contains (Jaeggi et al. 2018).

Figure 2.3 explains the emerging approach, which concentrates on the interplay between the dimensions and has been further evolved in the viable systems approach.

In this approach sustainability challenges, and economic challenges overlap. It therefore matters which objectives are strategically relevant and whether they focus—in the words of Mc Nelly—on impact or risk mitigation essentially. The difference between the two views requires different strategies as the as they cover largely different issues and aim for divergent objectives.

Impact investing, in its most consistent form follows an 'impact first' approach as delineated in the EVPA (2018) and operates within the Sustainable Development Goals Brest and Born (2013). Thereby, it can be delineated from ESG and negative screening approaches subsumed under 'finance first'. Probably the most common denominator is the proactive pursuance of social and/or environmental goals in the investment strategy instead of a passive strategy such as negative screening. In the portfolio engineering industry passive investment approaches cover 96% of all investments. In a passive investment approach there is no space for active pursuance of eco-social goals as the primary business objective. In addition, passively managed funds try to minimize the tracking error against the standard they use as a blueprint. This limits the leeway for integrating companies that focus on impact. Therefore impact investing can be found mainly in the actively managed alternative asset classes like private equity, venture capital and seed Dinnen and Beach (2018) Further, the investment evaluation in impact investing almost always incorporates an elaborative impact assessment as basis for an additional impact reporting like the Social Reporting Standard SRS (2018).

The impact analysis is core to any impact investment. The proactive approach of understanding if and how impact is generated by a venture is a key differentiator from environmental and social and governance (ESG) screening approaches used in the traditional sustainability models (Dinnen & Beach 2018). As part of the due diligence process, the insights from the impact analysis are crucial to the ultimate investment decision. Further, the analysis identifies social key performance indicators (KPIs) in order to achieve measurability and traceability of the impact created.

Whereas ESG screening stems from the sources of so called sustainability rating agencies like Bloomberg, Sustainalitics, ISS Ethics, RobecoSam to name a few, that build the ESG scores on the Global Reporting Initiative framework (GRI 2020), using self-reported company sustainability reports and top it up with management interactions, Impact analysis stems from two different approaches: the Theory of Change and the logic model approach. According to Schober & Rauscher (2014, p. 7) who build upon Weiss (1995), "[...] the logic model reflects what is to be achieved [...], the theory of change focuses on the question how and under what preconditions specific effects are to be achieved [...]". Moreover they highlight the importance of empirical evidence upon which the assumptions for a systematic change through certain interventions are built. The main elements of an impact analysis which is investment decision relevant consists of (1) understanding and analysing the eco-social challenge, reduce complexity (for instance using the Cynefin framework), expose causal links and interpret the ventures activities in context of the SDGs and the societal challenges it is addressing accordingly and (2) having described the societal issue as well as the causal links of a social venture's business activities addressing it, we then summarize these findings and give an outlook of what is ought to be achieved using the IOOI-Logic-Model (IOOI = Input, Output, Outcome, Impact).

2.2 The Emerging Role of Taxonomies

Using the EU Action Plan for Sustainable Growth (EU, 2019) the EU with its proactive approach of defining target industries and target technologies, and its intention to redirect capital to sustainable growth, the EU decided for an impact based approach rather than a risk based approach using the emerging model of sustainability. The EU has published Its EU Action Plan containing a green, a brown and a social taxonomy, the EU Green Bond, 2 climate benchmarks, the Sustainable Finance Disclosure Regulation (SFDR) and the Social Economy Action Plan in the year 2019–2021, In the EU definition an asset is ownly sustainable, when it fulfils one of the environmental or social objectives defined by the EU the green taxonomy or the social taxonomy enshrined in the directives, a social taxonomy is underway), does not harm any of the other eco-social objectives (Do No Significant Harm) and applies to good governance practices as defined by the OECD norms based screening. This latter art is the risk assessment part, however the main focus (key objectives plus DNSH) is on the key objectives to be achieved in future and only then rounded up by a ESG screening (OECD norms based) and has its basis in creating an ecosocial impact. As Fig. 2.4 depicts a sustainability assessment according to the EU requires three steps: First of all, the positive impact to the environment or the social impact have to be fulfilled as defined by the EU Green taxonomy and its classification criteria. In a second step it has to be ensured that there is no harm provided by the activities of this asset, company or project to other environmental or social goals and finally there has to be a screening on fulfilling ESG criteria based . To differentiate impact and ESG please turn to Sect. 2.3.

The EU has been working on its taxonomies for more than 5 years and got advice from a counsel of asset providers, asset managers and Civil society Organization and Universities the so called High Level Expert Groups. But it is not just the EU that is

Fig. 2.4 Own representation: Definition of Sustainability

developing its taxonomy. Taxonomies have come to be developed and are emerging as sustainable finance classification systems all around the world. Market- based efforts have reflected a sectoral and project-based methodology in line with the approach of the sustainable finance market. Many countries, so the political official sector has developed taxonomies, in some cases based on identifying green and/ or sustainable activities building on classification systems developed for statistical and economic analysis purposes (ICMA, 2021). Official sector taxonomies may incorporate additional considerations beyond classification purposes, such as requirements to consider multiple sustainable objectives or to avoid conflicting aims (like e.g. the EU "do no signicant harm"requirement), as well as to take into account social criteria (ICMA, 2021). The International Capital Market Association (ICMA) as a main market player has likewise developed requirements for successful taxonomies.

They propose some key success factors for taxonomies with the objective of promoting international consistency and market usability. Taxonomies should be:

- Targeted in their purpose and objectives.
- Additional in relation to existing international frameworks.
- Usable by the market for all intended purposes.
- Open and compatible with complementary approaches and initiatives.
- Transition-enabled incorporating trajectories and pathways.

Taxonomies define and explain how to develop them to provide clear guidance to the market on what activities, assets and/or projects are eligible as green (and increasingly as transitional) and or social. The progress made on the EU Taxonomy further accelerated the discussion about taxonomies all over the world.

A "taxonomy" is a classification system identifying activities, assets, and/or project categories that deliver on key climate, green, social or sustainable objectives with reference to identified thresholds and/or targets. Some introduce eligibility criteria that can be quantitative (e.g., absolute and relative performance thresholds) or qualitative and process based. Others only list and describe the projects, assets, activities based on an assessment of their sustainability. (ICMA 2021).

The author herewith provides an overview over these taxonomies with the aim to catalyse whether they might be helpful in streamlining impact investing.

The EU Action Plan for Sustainable Growth and the EU Taxonomy

The EU Action Plan Financing Sustainable Growth (hereafter Action Plan) he 2018 Action Plan centered on developing the **EU Taxonomy**, putting in place disclosure regimes in particular the Sustainable Finance Disclosure Regulation (SFDR), and developing tools for the market to develop sustainable investment solutions and prevent greenwashing.

It includes the introduction of two climate benchmarks, the SFDR accounting and the consideration of sustainability in the supervisory regulations for banks and insurance companies, which includes the 'Green Supporting Factor'. At its heart is a unified classification system of economic activities, called a taxonomy, which aims to end the fragmentation, fraying and fragmentation of the concept of sustainable or green investments. The taxonomy defines a methodology, as well as quantitative and qualitative screening criteria. The Taxonomy has now developed such screening criteria for 67 activities in seven key sectors. Taxonomy lists technical criteria and defines requirements for sustainable companies, investments, projects and funds. It contains a clear description of which investments, companies, project and assets are to be considered sustainable in the sense of the EU sustainability definition. So far, the basic framework of the technical taxonomy is in place, as well as a well-developed Green Bond Standard, which contains the requirements for registration as an "EU Green Bond". Taxonomy, Green Bond Standard as well as climate benchmarks and climate accounting is completed. An important part of the package is the governance structure. The agreement provides for an independent platform for sustainable finance (Platform for Sustainable Finance) to develop and maintain the full taxonomy. The EU has launched the International Platform for Sustainable Finance (IPSF) with third countries and plans to establish the stand-alone Sustainable Infrastructure Europe by end of 2020. The taxonomy is flanked by the Disclosure Regulation, which applies from 2021 onwards. According to the EU Commission's Green Infrastructure Strategy, ecosystems and biodiversity must be preserved. Ecosystems provide services for the benefit of society. The approach has evolved in international fora from biodiversity to preservation of ecosystems services. This will be implemented by the EU according to its Green Infrastructure Strategy through Sustainable Infrastructure Europe.

In order to meet the EU's climate and energy targets for 2030 and reach the objectives of the European green deal, the EU regards it vital to direct investments towards sustainable projects and activities (EU Taxonomy, 2020).

With the taxonomy, climate benchmarks and the supporting mechanisms, the EU wants to create a single market for sustainable finance and a uniform classification system for environmentally sustainable economic activities (EU Taxonomy, 2020). The EU defines six objectives in its green taxonomy: climate change mitigation, climate adaptation risk mitigation, sustainable use of water and marine resources, circular economy, pollution prevention and healthy ecosystems (see Fig. 2.5).

The eligibility criteria required for the CCM (climate change management) objective under Annex 1 of the Climate Delegated Act are very diverse. Some low-carbon (e.g., renewable energy generation from solar and wind) and enabling activities (e.g., manufacturing of low- carbon technologies) are considered eligible and substantially contributing to the CCM by their very nature and without performance thresholds, but indeed subject to the Do No Significan Harm (DNSH) objective. For other activities, especially the transitional ones, the Substantial Contribution depends on the satisfaction of GHG performance thresholds and/or various process-based requirements (due diligences and verification).

Regarding the climate change activities (CCA) objective, an activity needs to provide an adaptation solution either for itself or enable the adaptation of people,

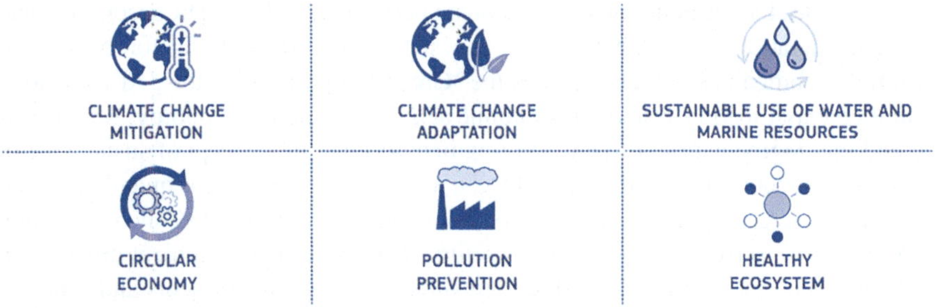

Fig. 2.5 EU Green Deal Targets as basis for the green taxonomy

nature, or assets. This approach is comparable with the Climate Bonds Initiative Climate Resilience Principles where the adaptation can be asset-focused or system-focused. The location and context-specific nature of climate adversities and avoiding adverse impact on other activities, people, nature, and assets also need to be considered. The Substantial Contribution for CCA under Annex 2 of the Climate Delegated Act, on the other hand, are qualitative and quite standard across most activities. These require the implementation of physical and non-physical solutions that substantially reduce the material physical risks based on the identification of the latter from an indicative list of climate- related hazards (included as an appendix) and with an assessment that is proportionate to the scale and expected lifespan of the activity. Also, among other requirements, nature-based, green, or "blue" adaptation solutions should be favoured to the extent possible, and consistency with overarching adaptation efforts as well as regular monitoring of solutions should be ensured. It is also important to note that the Annex 2 on the CCA includes some specific adaptation- enabling activities (e.g., engineering, financial and insurance services, etc.) as well as activities that provide essential services and solutions like health, education and arts (ICMA, 2021).

The green taxonomy is complemented by the forthcoming social taxonomy, (report on social taxonomy expected by the end of 2022), a uniform classification system for socially sustainable activities and the Social Economy Action Plan. Together with the brown taxonomy and the SFDR reporting, they form the EU Taxonomy of sustainable activities (Morningstar, 2021).

On July sixth, the European Commission published its Strategy for Financing the Transition to a Sustainable Economy, the successor of the EU's Sustainable Finance Action Plan, which launched in 2018. The strategy focuses on transforming the financial system and financing transition plans, building on the 2018 Action Plan, which centered on developing the EU Taxonomy, putting in place disclosure regimes, and developing tools for the market to develop sustainable investment solutions and prevent greenwashing.

The new strategy identifies four main areas for action for the financial system to fully support the transition to a sustainable economy:

1. **Financing the transition**: tools and policies to finance transition plans and reach climate and other environmental goals

2. **Inclusiveness**: access to sustainable finance for individuals and small and medium companies
3. **Financial sector resilience and contribution**: support the financial sector to contribute to meeting the EU's Green Deal targets, becoming resilient, and combat greenwashing
4. **Global ambition**: collaborating globally and promote an ambitious global sustainable finance agenda

Together with the new strategy, the Commission also published the rules for how and when companies ('non-financial undertakings') and financial institutions ('financial undertakings') need to do their Taxonomy-related reporting, the Delegated Act for Taxonomy Regulation in particular articles, 7, 8 and 9 (EU Delegated Act, 2021). The EU Taxonomy also promotes the life cycle assessment of activities wherever possible and requires compliance with a social dimension by undertakings with reference to international texts and conventions. The usability of the EU Taxonomy is a major topic of debate given that it is cross-referenced in many other regulations and policies, and the International Platform on Sustainable Finance (IPSF) has a dedicated group working on the subject. Firstly, companies subject to the Non-Financial Reporting Directive (NFRD) in Europe, generally large public companies, will disclose to what extent their business activities align with the EU Taxonomy in terms of turnover, CapEx, and OpEx as of 2022 for the CCM and CCA objectives. Asset managers will also disclose the proportion of alignment of their sustainability-focused products. Secondly, the EU Taxonomy will become the main reference for regulated sustainable financial products in Europe like the EU Green Bond (ICMA, 2021).[1]

Through this new strategy and the unified classification system creating a standard and classification, it might be possible in the future to apply eco-social dimensions as listing criteria on an impact stock exchange or an impact segment on a traditional stock exchange. For instance the IPSF has currently a dedicated workstream led by the EU and China to develop a "Common Ground Taxonomy". The outcome of this workstream is expected to be released in 2021 (ICMA, 2021).

Asian Taxonomies: China, Malaysia, Singapore and others

In China, the official sector guidelines on eligible projects for green bonds can be traced back to 2015 when two sets of standards prevailed in the market. The Green Bond Endorsed Project Catalogue (2015 Edition) ("2015 Project Catalogue") published by the China Green Finance Committee, an organisation supported by the People's Bank of China (PBOC), applied to all types of green bonds in China[8],

[1]The EU explains the application of the classification criteria in ist Green Bonds Usabiity Guide https://ec.europa.eu/info/sites/default/files/business_economy_euro/banking_and_finance/documents/200309-sustainable-finance-teg-green-bond-standard-usability-guide_en.pdf.

except green enterprise bonds which were regulated by the National Development and Reform Commission (NDRC)'s Guideline for Issuing Green Bonds referred to as "2015 Guideline"(China National Development and Reform Commission). In 2019 Peoples Bank of China and the national energy administrator published a catalogue of green industries, the Green Industry Guidance Catalogue 2019 Edition i.e. the "2019 Industry Catalogue"(China National Development and Reform Commission). As the name indicates, the 2019 Industry Catalogue identifies a concise list of industries considered green in China. Following this achievement in harmonising domestic definition of green, the three regulators—PBOC, NDRC and CSRC—announced in April 2021 that they will work on creating standards for climate finance and striving for international harmonisation of green bond standards as the next steps (ICMA, 2021).

Malaysia's central bank, Bank Negara Malaysia (BNM), issued a discussion paper on Climate Change and Principle-based Taxonomy in December 2019 and finalised it as a guidance document in April 2021, creating a classification system for assessing economic activities that promote transition towards a low carbon and climate resilient economy.

The taxonomy will apply to licensed banks, investment banks, Islamic banks, insurers and reinsurers, operators, and prescribed development financial institutions under the supervision of BNM. Malaysia's taxonomy is principally designed for financial institutions to classify the assets in their lending and investment portfolios, measure the climate-related risks and exposure, and report to BNM, for internal risk management and supervisory purposes. It provides a framework for Financial Institutions to classify their assets into categories related to climate transition (See flowchart below). The level of climate-friendliness ranges from category C1 ("climate supporting") to C2 and C3 ("transitioning") to C4 and C5 ("watchlist"). Figure 2.6 The Flowchart illustration the classification process of the BNM taxonomy. They start with the guiding questions whether or not the facility contributes positively or negatively to climate change or climate change mitigation measures, apply a DNSH provision and if yes look at the remedy measures the facility has taken to reduce the negative impacts.

More taxonomies are in the making that are led or supported by the official sector, for instance by Bangladesh, Mongolia, Singapore, and South Africa. It is acknowledged that other countries, such as Australia, Canada, and Colombia, are currently developing their taxonomies, but as they have not published any progress reports or revealed information about the design or usage yet.

Differences and commonalities of Taxonomies and their usability for Impact Investing Transactions.

Taxonomies are on the rise and looking for a harmonized classification system and needs to be criteria. While the criteria and frameworks are far from identical, there are some compelling patterns that can help finding universal listing criteria for Impact Investments.

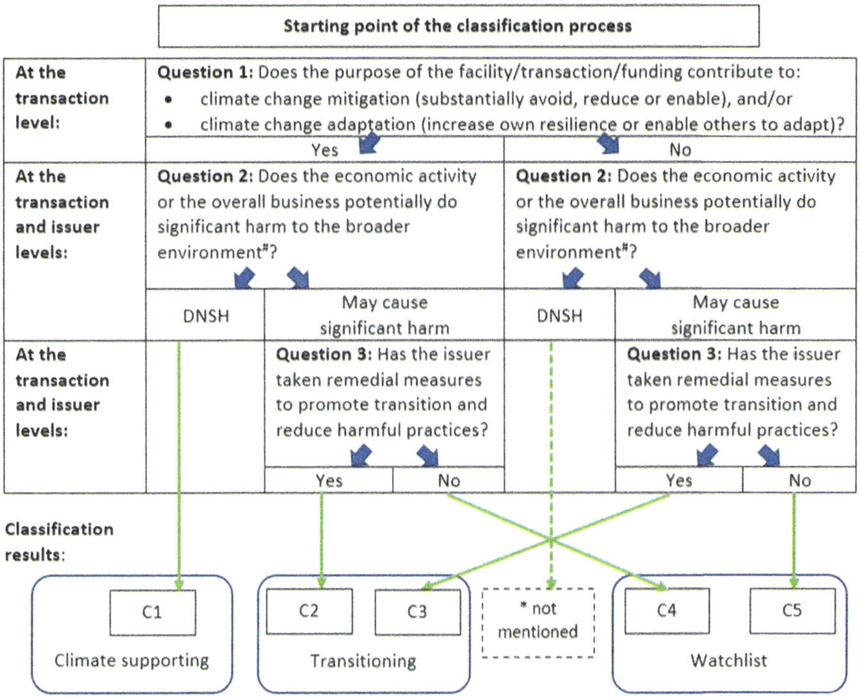

Fig. 2.6 The flow of the taxonomy

2.3 Impact Investing Versus ESG Approaches

The demand for investments that pro-actively combine desired social or environmental impact and financial returns is growing (Global Impact Investing Network GIIN, 2016a, 2016b). Given the recent upsurge in entrepreneurship (Fairlie et al., 2015; OECD, 2016; Schwabel, 2017), shifting attitudes towards the role of business in society (Deloitte, 2016), and a broad policy push for sustainable development (UN, 2015; UNFCCC, 2015). There should also be no shortage of investors and financiers eager to absorb this demand. The problem, as emphasized both by the World Economic Forum and UNEPFI (WEF 2013; UNEPFI 2017), lies in matching assets that create positive impacts with investors in a manner that is efficient, effective, transparent, and scalable (WEF 2013). In other words, redirecting investment and finance, to impact oriented investments compatible with the UN Sustainable Development Goals (SDG), the EU Taxonomy and the Paris Agreement is a key factor in turning around the investment philosophy. The same applies to the process of growing impact assets and supporting entrepreneurs in their search for capital when they grow beyond the venture capital or private equity phase. Both factors (access of entrepreneurs to a liquid impact investing marked) plus the potential to grow impact investing out of the private equity/venture capital niche are crucial for making the 'impact economy' (Martin, 2016) grow exponentially rather than linearly (WEF 2013).

Today impact investing is mostly the domain of wealthy individuals, foundations, and family offices (Kleissner, 2019). Institutional investors like pensions funds are not yet able to meaningfully participate in this new manner of investing for a number of (several) legal and governance restrictions like for instance MIFIS II (Kleissner, 2019; Wendt, 2017; Wendt 2020). This is not just because of a lack of products, but rather a lack of access to products available to more affluent(ial) investors, and a lack of adequate transaction platforms (Kleissner, 2019).

The author provides a detailed analysis on the various definitions of impact investing, its perceived inconsistencies and shortcomings which may also influence the efficiency and effectiveness of SSEs or ISEs and what Impact stock exchanges based on different definitions may or may not be capable of providing. If the definition is not clear it is obvious that stock exchanges first of all have the freedom to find their own definition, thereby sculpture the market, find their own (strong or weak) listing criteria, define what is impact and whether and how it needs to be measured or at least defined, and may preclude a transparent market where impact investments can be transferred between stock exchanges and where investors can compare like with like. Therefore a lack of a clear definition of impact investing has a domino effect. It will not be clear then what needs to be assessed in an impact assessment, how it needs to be assessed based on what criteria and with what outcomes. This could constitute a clear hindrance of a global market and will allow both investors, investees and SSEs to be in the business of cherry picking, definition picking, assessment picking leaving a scattered patchwork map of impact investing where investments cannot be compared based on impact assessment, impact reports and impact criteria definition and measurement. Please turn to Sect. 2.6 for a in depth discussion on the inconsistencies of impact investing.

For this publication impact investing is defined as investing in companies, that proactively integrate social or environmental return within a business model and investment strategy, normally using a lock-step approach (Brest and Born 2013). The integration of social and financial dimensions occurs within a business model as well as investment strategy and is commonly described double-bottom-line or lock-step approach. So a very important criterion is that the impact generating element cannot be taken out of the business strategy or the products as it is a key element of the product and the strategy itself. It has become part of the DNA of the company and the product line. The definition therefore integrates the environmental and social dimensions into the DNA of the business model and strategy ex-ante instead of filtering and mitigating undesired impacts of a business model ex post and thereby clearly differentiates itself from Environmental and Social Governance concept (ESG). It was the European Security and Markets Authority ESMA which called the ESG approaches inconsistent and needing harmonization (ESMA 2019). As an example we can compare EXXON Mobile to Tesla. The Environmental and Social Governance that Exxon Mobile executes very diligently, does not change the underlying of their strategy and product line. Exxon Mobile might rank high on ESG, but there is no impact on their business model and products. They still produce and refine oil, gas and other natural ressources. On the other hand when we look at Tesla, they have a horizon 3 innovation product, a new way of driving. Do they have a positive impact on society, climate with their product. Eventually, – when we use an entire value chain analysis from extracting licium out of the earth (with its human rights and soil karstification up to the recycling of the batteries may be not)—but at least we have a product that claims to have a positive impact, which still needs to be analysed in an impact assessment and applying measurement criteria. Would Tesla fulfill the Do No Significant Harm Criterion in the EU Definition and does it apply consistent ESG criteria like EXXON Mobil, does Tesla have a good governance? This is anyone's guess. The example however shows that ESG does not influence the underlying and is most of the time ex-post reporting and measurement of the reporting success, whereas impact investing wants to solve a environment or societal problem using market mechanisms including innovation and product and strategy design. It therefore has an ex ante perspective, which of course needs then to be materialized by criteria assessment, management and measurement. The definition f impact criteria, conduct of impact assessments and impact reporting and measurement is not trivial as the example of Tesla shows. For more information on impact criteria, impact assessments, reporting and measurement please turn to Sect. 2.6.

The definition we use for impact investing further allows us to align with the EU Action Plan for Sustainable Growth and in particular the EU Taxonomy, which defines a positive list for green investments (The Green Taxonomy) and will in future create a list of social investments (The Social Taxonomy). The EU created a list of businesses creating negative impacts needing mitigation (The Brown Taxonomy). When looking into the future of redirecting capital to Sustainable Growth (EU Action Plan, 2019), it is not enough to mitigate negative impacts of the business model, but rather create a business model that has positive eco-social effects and financial return as part of the business strategy and model itself. Providing a positive eco-social impact is not yet always at the core of the ESG aligned business model. Traditional business models are decided first, the ESG mitigation strategy next. The lock-step approach leads to a situation where the eco-social return is part of the value chain and product and cannot be taken out. While oil industry companies have extensive and compulsory ESG procedures and sustainability reports according to the Global Reporting Initiative (GRI), they are still in the business of oil production. So, they would fall into the Brown Taxonomy of the EU Action Plan and not be considered as impact investing per definition– independent on how good their sustainability reporting and mitigation strategy may be. The impact definition aligns with the Global Impact Investors Network (GIIN), which defines Impact investments as "investments made with the intention to generate positive, measurable social and environmental impact alongside a financial return" (Global Impact Investing Network GIIN, 2016a, 2016b, 2016c).

The impact investing industry is still very heterogeneous and inconsistent with regard to its practices. The most common denominator we focus on is the *proactive* pursuance of social and/or environmental goals in the investment strategy instead of a passive strategy such as negative screening (Brest and Born 2013). Further, the investment evaluation in impact investing almost always incorporates an elaborative impact assessment as basis for an additional impact reporting (ibid). Components of impact investment and their use in ISE/SSE listing criteria have been analysed in our

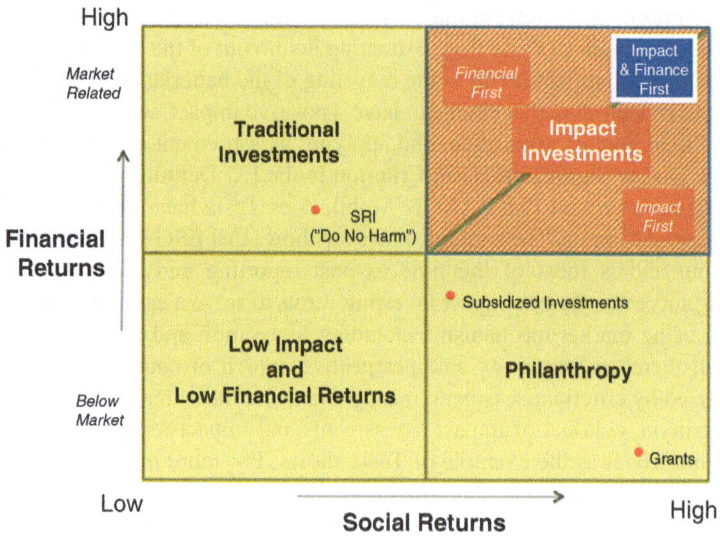

Fig. 2.7 Impact Investing own presentation

literature review to find out to what extent ISEs/SSEs live up to impact creation requirements. Not all do. We therefore believe that these components turned into listing criteria can create a level playing field for putting impact investments on stock exchanges.

The field of impact investing is populated by different classes of investors as shown in Fig. 2.7 below. Impact first investors, those prepared to forgo an a marginal unit of additional profit for a marginal unit of impact (often foundations, endowments) and those who according to their mandate and fiduciary duties will focus on financial profit first. Impact first, financial first investors will not compromise on either. Integral investors are also part of the impact and financial first segment (GIIN, 2016b).

Impact investments may fit in a 2 × 2 matrix. Impact first and financial first are in the upper left and lower right quadrants, implying a trade-off. In the lower left quadrant, we have deals with suboptimal financial and impact returns—an investor wouldn't make these types of investments. In the upper right quadrant, we have those investments that achieve risk-adjusted rates of financial returns and strong social and environmental impact. These are the impact assets, investors will like to go for.

GIIN states that "A theory of change (also referred to as the Theory of Value Creation or Logic Model) is an expression of the sequence of cause-and-effect, actions or occurrences by which organizational and financial resources are hypothesized to be converted into the desired social and environmental results (GIIN, 2016c). A Theory of Change provides a conceptual road map for how an organization expects to achieve its intended impact and is often displayed in a diagram (GIIN,

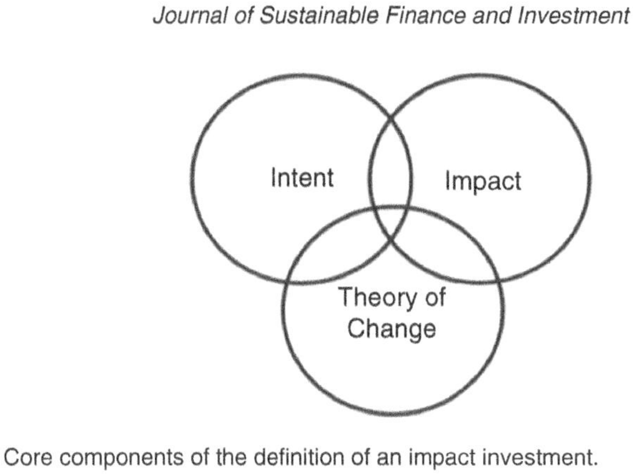

Fig. 2.8 Impact Investing and its intertwining with Theory of Change (Jackson, 2013)

2016c)." A Theory of Change can often be expressed as an if-then statement, specifying what the organization does and its expected results"(GIIN, 2016c). It has recently be argued that such a Theory of Change provides a clear framework for measuring, tracking and improving impact. The rationale of the Theroy of Change is to shift the focus from design to successful implementation and circumscription of the desired social and environmental outcome. The theory of change allows to build the transformation journey from intent to impact (Fig. 2.8).

2.4 The Perceived Need of Impact Stock Exchanges or Social Stock Exchanges

The Word Econmic forum has made the claim for impact investing in 2013 in its From the margin to the mainstream report (WEF 2013). According to a number of academics and practitioners the fundraising is done via crowdfunding, start up pre-seed and seed capital and the investors are mainly High Net-Worth Individuals (HNWI), foundations and venture capitalsts (Colasanti et al., 2020; McWade, 2012; Kleissner 2018).

According to Mendell and Nogales (2009), eco-social entrepreneurs seeking investment are confronted with out-dated categories and schemes (e.g. the demand for more bank guarantees, track record). Therefore, as indicated by the same authors, a cultural adaptation is needed first of all of the financial communities and then of the legal, accounting and political communities at both national and international level. These aspects do not yet reflect the findings of the pre-study (Wendt 2020), where institutional investors are also struggeling with the low lot size which make it impossible for them to invest under the MIFID 2 rules and the lack of market making.

Whereas the Forbes Magazines stated in 2014 "As the spotlight on investors seeking social investments continues to brighten, the rise of social (impact) stock exchanges—places where people can buy shares in businesses with missions that align with theirs—shouldn't be all that surprising" (Forbes, 2014). However, in reality Institutional Investors have little to no impact investments in their portfolios. The creation of ISEs/SSEs is an "expensive and long-term market building venture," (OECD, 2014) and represents an important aspect of this more general process of discursive and institutional development. Therefore, SSEs or ISEs need to be defined and designed in a way that fulfils the requirements not just of family offices, venture capitalists, foundations, seed investors and HNWI, but also Institutional Investors. Currently the scenery resembles a Garage Lab scenario with a scattered ecosystem with few scalable projects and the continued importance of more traditional forms of funding rather than a fully-fledged ISE/SSE scenario which can be characterized as 'social innovation boom', accompanied by large volumes of private and institutional investment and the emergence of a broad spectrum of financial instruments and actors, including fully developed ISEs/SSEs, successfully operating in the context of sophisticated regulatory and institutional standards.

A fully operational ISE/SSE or a new special market segment at existing stock exchanges would need to perform a variety of functions, such as intermediation, bring new issues to market, providing liquidity and marketability to existing impact securities, price impact securities, ensure safety of transactions, contribute to impact economic growth, spreading an impact equity cult, attract new investors, provide clear impact driven listing criteria, provide training to companies in regulatory and compliance issues, provide market making and enough liquidity thus offering the opportunity for investors to disinvest and have a clear on-boarding process for new securitized impact investments (Wendt 2020).

The pre-study of Wendt 2020 shows that institutional investors have requirements towards ISEs/SSEs in order to make them efficient and effective. The following requirements have been cited as necessary prerequisites for a functioning ISE/SSE, which deviate from the shape that ISEs/SSEs are taking to day.

In the pre-study conducted by Wendt (2020) results highlight some shortcomings, the most important ones are summarized here (4 out of a list of 11). The following issues have been criticized about existing ISEs /SSEs.

ISEs/SSEs have

- no blueprint in design of ISEs/SSEs that draw from traditional exchanges
- not high enough lot-size to allow Institutional Investors to participate
- are peer to peer platforms with no market making,
- do not have global standardization nor harmonization of listing criteria.

Blueprint, peer to peer lending and lack of market making can be circumscribed as design issues. Missing lot size could be an expression of a deeper market failure which needs to be removed.

Knowing what blocks institutional investors for investing proportionally in impact, although this is in their mandate (for many like the Norwegian Pension Fund) is relevant in order to make suggestions on design and implementation and to understand how the blockages how the blockages can be removed.

BlueOrchard recently found, that impact investing can be an interesting solution for pension funds in particular, their challenge is finding investment opportunities that support their return targets and meet a number of other sustainability requirements. In addition, they are often looking for ways to diversify away from existing asset classes in their portfolios. Impact investing can be an attractive way for pension funds to incorporate sustainability requirements into their investments while also providing diversification benefits.

2.5 The Current State of SSEs and ISEs

Looking at the current structure of impact stock exchanges ISEs (often referred to as Social Stock Exchanges or SSEs) it turns out, that they are separate from the huge stock exchanges, apply in most cases a peer-to-peer lending approach with a direct investor/ investment matching. The impact investing stock exchanges are platforms without market makers, with little volume and liquidity. While it might be interesting for venture capitalists and private equity investors to further pursue their idiosyncratic approach to impact investing, the differences in approach might be good for the impact investor, but fall short to grasp the full scaling opportunity of impact investing. What is good on the micro-level might constitute market failure on the meta-level. The scaling of impact investments will need liquidity, access to liquid marketplaces where mainly professional investors invest and market making takes place instantly (Wendt 2020; Wendt, 2017). The success of impact is not mainly in creating a viable business model and impact, but in multiplying and scaling the impact as effectively as possible. Time to market is one key component in this rush for assets and capital (Wendt 2020; Wendt, 2017).

The creation of regulated funding platforms separate or integrated in the existing stock exchanges has been proposed as a necessary step towards democratizing and popularizing impact investing, easing the asset search process for investors and capital access for entrepreneurs (Forbes, 2014). A more recent survey by Barclays (2017) found that despite the widespread interest in the topic, very few investors have actually made impact investments. The ISEs/SSEs are not to be confounded with the UN initiative on Sustainable Stock Exchanges which is motivating existing stock exchanges to better integrate ESG into their procedures in a multi-stakeholder dialogue since 2009. The results after 10 years are mixed and did not foster impact investing after 10 years of existence and the alignment or harmonization of the 104 exchanges is difficult. Moreover, the European Market and Security Authority ESMA has criticized the lack of comparability between ESG approaches and has called for better and more consistent ESG disclosure. Reliable and relevant information on ESG factors is needed to respond to changing investor preferences, but also to ensure that these factors are considered when assessing the risks, returns and value of investments. Therefore, one of the questions is whether it is effective and efficient for capital allocations and scaling, that ISEs/SSEs exist as pure platforms separate from the stock market. It is a fact, that Institutional Investors are absent on these platforms and although they express the wish to invest in impact only very few have. This raises the question of market failure.

Impact Stock Exchanges/Social Stock Exchanges (ISX/SSX) developed to address some of the outdated structures, over the years. Some authors see their potential in becoming alternative or complementary financial institutions (Galina et al. 2013a, b; Wendt, 2017) or even may develop into an integration at existing stock exchanges.. ISXs/SSXs intermediate between eco-social enterprises, to match investors and investees (Wendt 2020) and wish to help raise capital to finance through a direct investor-investee maching. ISXs/SSXs have been founded with the idea that there are enough investors around who are willing to invest their money in projects with social and environmental outputs (Calderini et al., 2018). The matching is found to possibly maximise the eco-social value of investments according to some authors (Pavlov, 2017; Wendt, 2017). However, as pointed out by many authors, there is no consensus on the infrastructures, definitions, processes, listing or accreditation criteria and tools that ISEs/SSE can provide for entrepreneurs and investors (Mendell & Nogales, 2009; Pavlov, 2017; Secinaro et al., 2019, Wendt 2020). A nascent stream of literature is focusing on ISEs/SSEs, however the area of research does not include institutional investors view and experience, nor a useful analytical systematisation of ISEs/SSEs, their strengths and shortcomings. Wendt (2017) provided a historic systematization, however there is currently no comparison of what the listing criteria on the exchanges entail and how the investment process works. Calandra and Favareto (2020) were the first to analyse definitions, process and structures, however even their analysis based on a literature review cannot entirely reveal the listing requirements, which are not made transparent by the exchanges themselves. It follows that listing requirements and the entire design of stock exchanges still needs to be investigated in order to optimize and harmonize the successful approaches. The issue may even go deeper and it needs to be looked at through the lenses of those powerful investors which are absent: Institutional Investors (Wendt 2020).

To start with, researcher uses a literature review to collect what is known to date about this emerging field in order to review, to classify and extract, through academic and professional databases, information on the field of ISEs/SSEs.

As suggested by some authors the definition of ISEs/SSEs is still varying (Calandra and Favareto 2020, Wendt (2020). The differing ways of defining ISXs/SSXs may cloud the impact measuring, monitoring and finally impact creation process and lead to embezzlement of Institutional Investors. It does not help solve the idiosyncratic way in which impact investing is done. The approaches of ISEs/SSEs appear to be as idiosyncratic as the social enterprises and the field of impact investing. As Brest and Born (2013) pointed out guiding the investment decision, setting up the impact reporting and the impact analysis or even impact assessment is key in the communication to the investors. It also helps to attract new investors who look for impact investment approaches that are more proactive than, for instance, negative screening approaches. Hence, it signals credibility in the field of impact investing (Brest and Born 2013). Further, the investment evaluation in impact investing almost always incorporates an elaborative impact assessment as basis for an additional impact reporting (Brest and Born 2013). So far there appears to be agreement, that somehow the impact should be described, assessed and monitored via reporting. Although there is agreement on the first version, deepening the analysis, it is possible to realise how many descriptions are present today. This substantial uncertainty is partly due to the situation of uncertainty, also at the level ISXs/SSXs around the world. The original plans for the constitution of the ISXs/SSE have undergone variations due to the lack of interest on the part of the stakeholders involved in the use of the instrument. This shows according to various authors the uncertainty and lack of clarity on the use of ISEs/SSEs definition, if not design (Glänzel 2014, Bishop & Green, 2015).

This un-clarity has initiated discussions of professionals on the necessity to define standards for the operation of these platforms. That is to say, specify whom they are designed for, what are the entry requirements, what is the necessary documentation to submit in order to obtain accreditation and then maintain membership.

Currently there is a variety of concepts the most successful models being the Impact Investment Network (U.K.), the Impact Investment Exchange (Singapore) and the Bolsa Social (Spain). In the follwoign literature review the author has concentrated on the design of these ISXs/SSEx as far as available including definition of the mission of the exchange, accreditation process, audience (investors) and Matching. Little is known about the impact measurement and reporting of these stock exchanges form their websites. They state that an annual impact reporting is required.

The theory of organisation has evolved by considering eco-social enterprises (S.E.s) as organisations often host projects of high social value (Battilana & Lee, 2014; Galaskiewicz & Barringer, 2012). For instance, these organisations could host microfinance organisations, sustainable food producers, labour companies and any other project of public importance. (Biancone et al., 2020; Dart, 2004; Dees, 2018; Mair, 2010; Mauksch et al., 2017; Steiner, 2016).

S.E.s are viewed as an innovative, and increasingly global, solution to bridge the service delivery gap of governments (Agapitova et al., 2017). ventures (Smith et al., 2013). Attracting investments seems to be one of the main problems of eco-social entrepreneurs. At the same time, some private investors are ready to invest their money, but they do need guarantees and want to be sure in economic and eco-social impact of these enterprises (Boguslavskaya & Demushkina, 2013). Some authors point out that ISEs/SSEs serves as a mediator between social enterprises, that need funding, and investors who are willing to invest their money (Boguslavskaya & Demushkina, 2013; Pavlov, 2017), Dadush, 2015a, 2015b. The history of SSE is not longer than 15 years. According to Boguslavskaya and Demushkina (2013), Pavlov (2017, 2019), SSEs create multiple advantages either for investors or for social enterprises and the community. Make the procedure of social-enterprise investment simpler (1), increase transparency of impact driven projects and companies (2), help to save time and cost of project searching (3), reduce the financial and administrative expenses (4), provide objective information about social projects placed on the exchange (5), increase the social value of investments (6), enable to obtain not only the financial but also the social impact of investment (7).

They also specified some advantages that ISXs/SSXs generate for social enterprises: create the opportunity to get investment (1), ensure stable functioning of the organisation (2), raise the value of their social activities (3), help to grow the company's value (4), increase company's recognisability and rating (5).

2.6 Review of Scientific Literature And Practitioners' View on SSEs

To create a map of what is known about ISXs/SSXs, the researchers used the literature analysis approach. In particular, the method makes it possible to investigate the primary scientific studies on specific topics (Paul & Criado, 2020). Therefore, the methodology used allows the analysis in different areas (Massaro et al., 2016).

The analysis was implemented using as keywords "Social Stock Exchange" and "Impact Stock Exchange". I focused on English items that were inherent to the searched object and used Scopus and Google Scholar as databases. Although in the social sciences Scopus returns a convincing result (Falagas et al., 2007; Mongeon & Paul-Hus, 2016), the reduced number of articles prompted me to continue the analysis also on Google Scholar for a more accurate study of the topic.

After an initial selection phase using databases, the researchers went on to consult the references of the articles found (i.e. snowball sampling) to increase further the sample being studied (Biancone et al., 2019; Lecy & Beatty, 2012). Further, the following search criteria were used: availability of the full text of the article (also by request to the author) (1), studies dealing with common stock exchange issues (2).

To verify the practices of professionals, I used a measurement technique based on electronic periodicals, expertly revised titles, consumer magazines, newspapers, news and blogs (Dal Mas et al., 2019; Massaro et al., 2018). Therefore, Ulrichsweb has been used to explore all data related to professionals (Meeks, 2018).

As soon as the scientific and academic sample was available, the titles and abstracts of both datasets were analysed to find out about definitions, accreditation process, audience and matching process. Subsequently, I came up with a final sample of study (Lecy & Beatty, 2012).

The results and method benefited from the PRISMA approach for the classification of results (Liberati et al., 2009). the research steps were as follows: Academic record identified through databases and snowballing, ($n = 530$), removal of duplicates, screening of records to find the criterions (definition, process, audience matching) and therefore 514 records had to be excluded. Sixteen articles remained and formed the universe of scientific articles that have been selected for the construction of the academic sample.

For the selection of professional contributions (practitioners), I used the filter "reviewed by experts". Compared to primary research with 7728 results, the application of the screen allowed evaluating 1637 results validated by experts in the field. After a careful selection, the researchers reached a final professional sample of 132 documents, websites, blogs and titles reviewed by experts.

Subsequently, I carried out the independent content analysis creating cognitive patterns (see categories) that allow the reader to visualise the items in a research flow (Flick et al., 2004). The first step was the reading of academic and professional contributions. Through the organisation phase, researchers built a matrix to test the paper's research question by identifying reading codes derived from the literature (Dal Mas et al., 2019; Secinaro et al., 2019).

Mapping the Functions of SSEs

The following paragraphs specify the academic and practical results identified. The variables under observation are definition (1), accreditation process (2), (3) audience (4) matching process.

The following tables summarize the view of practitioners and researchers found in the records about ISXs/SSXs.

Practitioners' View on Social Stock Exchanges/Impact Stock Exchanges

The highlight the functioning of the platforms it is important to understand how the founders conceived and designed the ISX/SSX and what problem they want to solve, how they want to solve it and how they circumscribe themselves as platforms, networks or regulated financial institutions. In this research I concentrate on the three ISXs/SSXs that are up and running successfully namely the Impact Investors Network (IIN) London, the IIX (Impact Investing Exchange in Singapore and the Bolsa in Spain. The following table provides a short overview on the different features, definition, mission, accreditation process (Table 2.1).

The author deducts form the analysis that the ISXs/SSXs are more incubation platforms than real stock exchanges and except for INN, who has a leg into the unregulated securitized asset market are dealing with the private investor or crowd that wants to do good. While the economic viability and visibility of the compact as an impact driver is important, in impact investing the impact can be multiplied by scaling the company, i.e. scaling the impact. The question arises whether these incubation platforms in their current form will allow the market to growth sufficiently the impact, to attract professional investors. Moreover the model for impact identification and measurement appears to be proprietary and nothing is known about the defining criteria, measurement and monitoring of impact, which could shy away more professional investors that are prwon in bid data analysis, customized

Table 2.1 Functions of SSEs

	INN/NEX (Impact Investing Network London in cooperation with NEX/now Aquis	IIX Impact Investing Exchange Singapore	Bolsa Impact Investing Exchange Spain
Mission (Website, press release)	IIN supports companies that join the network Scale and boost accredited impact investments through the partnership with Aquis which makes listing on the LSE possible Ideate more sustainable finance (press release 2009)	Help eco-social enterprises to find funding through the platform community Help potential investors (crowd) to identify, assess and invest into impact Social crowd-funding platform	Finance Companies with Growth Potential and generate positive impact on society and environment
Listing of Impact Assets possible on regulated Exchange	Yes through the cooperation with NEX, now Aquis, unlisted securities can enter the Growth segment of NEX and trade at the Londond Stock Exchange	No, Platform for matching investees and investors through Impact Partners, intermediaries and first point of contact between investors and investees. Who qualifies as Impact Partner not evident	No, platform provides direct matching for the crowd based on an AI mechanism.
Platform, Network or Institution	Network that cooperates with the regulated Aquis Stock Exchange Terms unknown Unregulated network with regulated partner	Platform with intermediation through so called impact partners Terms unknown	Incubation approach Platform with automated matching, First Spanish crowd-funding platform
Definition	INN supports companies that join the network and want to growth ethically and sustainably, after accreditation opportunity to receive investment from platform partners (like Aquis) Securities trading and exchange platform enabled through Aquis partner	Platform dedicated to companies with a eco-social mission and promotion of their impact activities Social Crowd-funding	The meeting point between companies with a social impact strategy and business plan and crowd investors
Accreditation Process	Organisations of different types may apply to become a network partner. Sound financials (track record and forecasts) plus good growth perspectives plus eco-social mission.	Online form: Companies applying must provide an impact report including core business criteria (business plan, impact achieved through activities) fulfil	Online Form: Financially sound organisation with good growth perspectives, Presentation of business model Screening of

(continued)

Table 2.1 (continued)

	INN/NEX (Impact Investing Network London in cooperation with NEX/now Aquis	IIX Impact Investing Exchange Singapore	Bolsa Impact Investing Exchange Spain
	Impact needs to be defined and an impact report provided as part of listing process. Impact Report to be provided on an annual basis. Criteria unknown Online Form, demonstrate impact, then contacted through the INN Business Development Team to discuss Impact Activities. Team also helps to prepare application and impact report Admission through the Impact Admission Panel Yearly impact reporting required Approach idiosyncratic and manually through business development team	investment readiness criteria, i.e. demonstrate they are Economically and financially sound Provide impact report annually Screening process through impact partners, they prepare a technical fact sheet and facilitate matching Approach idiosyncratic	application by internal team (criteria unknown) Announcement of company on dedicated page, promotion of company through events and establish contact to potential investors, investors may take part at events
Audience/ Investors	Private and through Aquis professional investors Retail and professional investors	Crowdfunding platform, retail investors	Crowd, retail investors
Matching Process	Through business development team	Through impact partners	AI based and through events, leveraging the Bolsa investors network
Activities of accredited members	Reduction of harmful emissions, energy efficiency, recycling, consultancy of social organisations, healthcare, education, eco-homes, sustainable mobility	Industrial and rural development, innovation technology, recycling, energy efficiency, social inclusion	Sustainable Fashion, Social Inclusion, efficiency, recycling, consultancy of social organisations, healthcare, education, sustainable mobility, responsible production

products and concepts, clear listing and measurement criteria. One more question arising is about whethr or nto a theory of change exists, as some authors claim measuring impact without having a theory of change will provide impossible. Likewise big companies listed at the stock market might be able to ideate, produce and implement a theory of change and whether they are left out as they might be reluctant to access such idiosyncratic platforms. It further appears that the price building mechanism on a platform with a small crew of investors only and low liquidity might not signal the right market price and pricing might be not build on the platform itself through an efficient bidding process but lie more in the area of negotiating with investors and consultants, which clearly reflects practices of incubators or venture capital organisations and not stock exchanges.

Academic View on Social Stock Exchanges/Impact Stock Exchanges

According to science stock exchange allows the democratisation of capital and can be defined as a meeting point between investors and social organisations, where they are able to promote impact investing controlled by impact investment boards and clearly defined criteria on which they are screened, evaluated and monitored investments using Environmental and Social Governance (Wendt, 2017). The newly developing taxonomies might add to finding clear criteria (see Sect. 2.5).

Many authors agree with Bernardino et al. (2016) and Moritz and Block (2016), these platforms are currently similar to a social crowdfunding model (also Belleflamme et al., 2014; Bernardino et al., 2016). According to Dadush (2015a, 2015b), social stock exchanges should be platforms designed to connect investors with social businesses in need of capital and serve as a mediator between enterprises and investors. It remains to be seen, whether they fulfil the function if mediation in an efficient and effective manner.

Adhana (2020) defined social stock exchange as a platform on which social enterprises, volunteer groups and welfare organisations are listed so that they can raise capital for the welfare of the society and the disadvantaged. The main aspect here is on capital raising, not financial investing with risk adjusted returns.

Analysing accreditation process, according to (Chaturvedi et al., 2019) only eco-social enterprises that have a track record of achieving measurable positive social and environmental impact should be listed as ISX/SSX. To be accepted, organisations need to comply impact and financial requirements. Impact requirements relate to the preparation of an impact report for at least a year by the listing entity, obtaining an impact certification by an independent body at least a year prior to listing and ensuring the primacy of social/environmental mission. Financial requirements would include meeting a minimum market capitalisation amount, publishing financial statements that meet specific specified standards at least a year before listing and demonstrating a financially sustainable business model (Chaturvedi et al., 2019).

Dadush (2015a, 2015b) stated that social stock exchanges need to fix specific admissions criteria for social businesses wishing to transact on their platform. Establishing requirements with which accredited members must comply to obtain and maintain their memberships, such as the production of financial and social reports. Is fundamental that companies must have "social or environmental impact as a core aim". To satisfy this requirement, companies must submit a Social Impact Report for review by the independent Admissions Panel composed of finance and impact-investing experts.

Concerning the areas of activity of accredited members, Pavlov (2017) mentioned they have to be social organisations that pursue a social mission & vision. This means they have social ends (primary goal) which generate revenues (secondary purpose) from their activity, like mainstream businesses, and they reinvest them internally to grow as firms, reaching more people in need.

These organisations are operating in different areas of business, but they must pursue a social objective (Bernardino & Freitas Santos, 2016).

Many authors have focus on food, security and agriculture (1), small business development (2), animal protection (3), education and health (4), environment and conservation (5), sustainable mobility (6), vulnerable people (7) (Bandini, 2014; Chaturvedi et al., 2019).

However these areas might be rearranged by the emerging taxonomies that create the legal framework for sustainable finance in many countries (see Sect. 2.5).

A short overview on the academic views on ISXs/SSXs is provided in (Table 2.2).

The approach adopted here is looking through the lenses of the scientist and the practitioner,which according to Romme et al. (2015), facilitates the dialogue between what is present in practice and what is studied by academics. The analysis of the results poses some interesting reflections.

First, despite the terminology, to date, social stock exchanges seem to be more similar to social crowdfunding platforms than real stock exchanges dedicated to buying and selling securities. The reference literature shown above confirms this. Moreover a number of exchanges have closed or are just existing on paper in some cases, the original project, related to the creation of social stock exchanges, didn't meet the interests of investors and social organisations. This reflection, therefore, opens the way for further research into why this model has not developed as much as the traditional market. According to Calandra and Favareto 2020 additional research by academics on this point is required in order to the creation of future models.

Table 2.2 Design requirements of ISXs/SSXs by Academics

Function of SSX mediation and visibility	Accreditation
The democratisation of capital (Wendt, 2017)	Impact and financial requirements (Chaturvedi et al., 2019)
Social crowdfunding (Bernardino et al., 2016, Moritz & Block, 2016)	Social mission & vision (Pavlov, 2017) Social objective (Bernardino & Freitas Santos
Platform designed to connect investors with social businesses in need of capital (Dadush, 2015a, 2015b)	Admissions criteria and requirements (Dadush, 2015a, 2015b)
The platform which allows investors to buy shares in social enterprises vetted by an official exchange (Adhana, 2020)	The sector of activities of social enterprises on the Social Stock Exchange (Bandini, 2014; Chaturvedi et al., 2019)

Another significant result obtained concerns the terminology used. The analysis among practitioners and academics showed that the professional world had devoted more interest to ISX/SSX than academics. As reported by Romme et al. (2015), this may be due to the difference in benefits and the immediate need of practitioners to provide solutions to a practical problem. Researcher through specific theoretical frameworks could verify the feasibility of the model used. Besides, further research is neededto see if there is a redesign of ISXs/SSXs is needed including an evolution of the impact business model in the future. Finally, the analysis of the academic and professional vision poses some points for reflection.

A key element is to understand whether the instrument of financial intermediation is effective and efficient and whether it could be relaunched by companies that own conventional stock exchanges.

2.7 Impact Investing

Addressing the Inconsistencies of Impact Investing

Institutional Investors, pension funds, insurance companies, asset managers and financial institutions and corporations—are increasingly challenged to allocate resources more effectively and efficiently to unmet eco-social needs whether for internal or external accounting and reporting. One of the challenges in accounting and reporting lies in assessing and aggregating eco-social impact across projects, stocks, programs, sectors, countries, regions and even time (Mudaliar et al. 2017a, b; Spiess-Knafl & Scheck, 2017; Taskforce, 2014).

The Global Impact Investors Network GIIN estimates that USD 502 billion have been invested in impact investment assets currently (Mudaliar & Dithrich, 2019). They see a growing market and interest in co-creating eco-social impact (henceforth used interchangeably with "social impact" or "eco-social impact"). Achieving eco-social and financial returns simultaneously through capital investments has placed social impact under much scrutiny regarding its accountability (Gray, 2010; Molecke & Pinkse, 2017; Nicholls, 2018).

Stakeholders are now all eager to find out how much impact this 502 billion USD has achieved before scaling investments (Lam & Tan, 2021). This creates currently a wait and see attitude. While conventional investments typically only adopt financial performance measurements to determine economic impact and efficiency, impact investing requires an integrated measurement system to account for economic and social impacts (Maas & Liket, 2011).

At a more fundamental level, the absence of a singular definition of "social impact" and how to measure it has generated immense confusion. For instance, in the impact investing community, output and operational performance metrics (not outcomes) are frequently used as claims for "impact" (Lam & Tan, 2021). There are also different jargons and theoretical frameworks employed by the various disciplines that critically examine impact assessment as a subject matter. This is largely due to the writers imposing the languages and perspectives of their respective fields on impact assessment practices in impact investing. (Lam & Tan, 2021).

Practitioners (private equity, venture capital, seed investors), advocates, researchers, critics, consultants, public organisations and academics—each of these groups tends to use their own impact assessment jargons and methodologies, that one which is familiar to them in their respective fields (Lam & Tan, 2021). Care and Wendt (2018) found diverging definitions of impact investing and diverging goals in their pre-study (Care & Wendt, 2018). As a result, there is often little attempt at addressing the critical differences in definitions (of what to create, how to create it) and methods for measurement (what and how to measure). This diversity in impact assessment approaches has been pointed out by a number of researchers (Bull, 2007; Ebrahim et al., 2014; Paton, 2003).

Discussion on the why, what and how of Impact assessment comes from a wide range of disciplines—including

(a) social accounting (Gibbon & Dey, 2011; Luke et al., 2013; Morgan, 2013),
(b) social finance (Chiappini, 2017; Nicholls et al., 2015),
(c) voluntary and non-profit (Arvidson & Lyon, 2014; Mook et al., 2015; Owen et al., 2015),
(d) business and management (Dufour, 2019; Molecke & Pinkse, 2017),
(e) organisational development and institutional legitimacy (Ebrahim et al., 2014),
(f) social entrepreneurship (Haski-Leventhal & Mehra, 2016; Ormiston & Seymour, 2011),
(g) evaluation (Hatry, 2013; Hoffman & Olazabal, 2018; Ruff & Olsen, 2018), economics and econometrics (Darby & Jenkins, 2006).
(h) Change management and programme theory development (Jackson & Harji, 2012; Jackson, 2013)
(i) Portfolio engineering and risk management (Brandstetter & Lehner, 2015; Brandstetter & Lehner, 2014)

Arising from the discussions in these fields are various nomenclatures, including: social performance management, performance measurement, social impact accounting, social impact measurement, impact evaluation, and program evaluation (Ebrahim & Rangan, 2014; Lall, 2019; Nicholls, 2018).

Many authors have pointed out the inconsistencies in approach to impact investing. Academic literature shows significant variations in the conceptualization of Impact Investing and authors highlight that Impact Investing goes by many names (Hebb, 2013; Höchstädter & Scheck, 2015; Rizzello et al., 2016) including double and triple bottom line, mission related investing, program-related investment, blended-value, and economically targeted investing.

Definitions of Impact Investing

While the least specific definition of impact investing[2] stems from Weber (2016a, 2016b) highlighting that the idea behind impact investing is that investors can pursue financial returns while also intentionally addressing social and environmental challenges. Weber and Feldmate argue that Impact Investing definitions are based on two common principles: (1) the blended value principle and (2) the principle of sustainable financial return (Weber & Feltmate, 2016a, 2016b). In this sense, Weber (2016a, 2016b) clarify that these two principles distinguish impact investment from conventional investment because the latter is not striving for positive social impact but only for financial return (Weber, 2016a, 2016b, p. 86). However, this definition needs some operationalization, as it leaves open the questions, what is impact, how shall it be achieved, how and what to measure and manage.

Brest and Born (2013) and (Lam & Tan, 2021) recently provided a clear outline of what impact investing needs to deliver:

1. **Additionality[3]:** some investors like the GIIN believe that impact investing should also incorporate the concept of 'additionality', which involves only allocating funds to businesses that they would not otherwise have chosen to invest in if they were not seeking to achieve a positive social impact. Development Finance Institutions (DFIs) are frequently asked to demonstrate their additionality—meaning that they make investments that the private sector alone would not—but additionality must be demonstrated. Evidence of additionality can however be inferred from observational investment data (Carter et al., 2018, Brest and Born 2013, Lam & Tan, 2021).
2. **Intentionality:** intentionality of creating social and/or environmental impact while generating financial returns - impact investors ought to articulate this as their mission or strategy in all their communications and use a lock-step approach (Brest and Born 2013, Lam & Tan, 2021).
3. **Evidenced based approach using impact data**: Secondly, impact investing is characterized as a practice whereby impact investors apply an evidence-based approach in designing impact through their investing to address specified unmet social or environmental needs. This means the impact design and measurement, with learning from impact data, are integral to both the pre-investment and post-investment processes—in deal flow generation, deal filtering, due diligence, deal

[2]The Rockefeller Foundation conceived the term "impact investing" at Bellagio in 2007. Impact investing is defined as "investments made into companies, organisations, and funds with the intention to generate measurable and beneficial social and environmental impact alongside a financial return (Network, 2019f).

[3]For example, general partners of an impact investment company could co-invest with international development agencies, government or quasi-government agencies as well as philanthropic organisations in a blended finance funding partnership. In this context, blended finance is the term given to the use of public or philanthropic capital to leverage private sector investment.

structuring, value creation, performance reporting and evaluation and deal exiting (Brest and Born 2013, Lam & Tan, 2021)

4. **Measurement:** impact investing is characterized by impact management and performance - the measuring, monitoring and evaluating of impact that is attributable to the investing (Brest and Born 2013, Lam & Tan, 2021). Some authors pointed out that measurement makes only sense when measuring alongside a theory of change or programme theory (Jackson & Harji, 2012)

Regarding the measurement of impact Clark et al. (2004) and Maas and Liket (2011) distinguish between input, action, output, outcomes, changes of social norms minus what would have happened anyway (impact) and goal alignment. Goal alignment allows to install feedback loops in the entire process of impact ideation, impact creation and helps distinguishing between output (x people vaccinated), outcomes (how did vaccination create societal change). The feedback loop based on goal alignment is to avoid the problem of mission drift. Using the prerequisites additionality, intentionality, evidence based lockstep approach data driven measurement and distinguishing between output coutcomes and impact (outcomes minus what would have happened anyway) aligns with the definition of the pioneers in the industry, namely the GIIN, the Rockefeller Foundation and the IFC and allows for fulfilling the criteria. We therefore use the definition from Clark et al. (2004) going forward. Using additionality means by definition impact investing can only happen on the primary market. However in order to help these investments to scale, allow efficient capital allocation, a price building mechanism, increased traction, liquidity, depth, width, immediacy and resiliency which all can come about with registration on a special segment at traditional stock exchanges. By listing these assets on the stock exchange they automatically become secondary market, however the logic that they would not have seen daylight if not investors in early phases had decided to invest because of intentionality which has led to a business model and strategy developed in a lock step approach. Going forward we therefore apply these four criteria above and the Impact Value Chain as guiding method for circumscribing impact investing (Fig. 2.9).

In this vein, it is important to define the what, the how and the measurement and reporting.

We define social impact in accordance with the Global Impact Investors Network GIIN and the Rockefeller Foundation as "the portion of the total outcome that happened as a result of the activity of an organisation, above and beyond what would have happened anyway" (Clark et al., 2004). In terms of levels of measurement and reporting, we make distinctions between:

1. Impact evaluation (which makes causal inferences on the results of an intervention through adequate control groups or baseline survey data)
2. Outcome evaluation (which offer valid indicators to tests for change in social behavior or improved conditions)
3. Output reporting (which is akin to performance tracking of planned activities

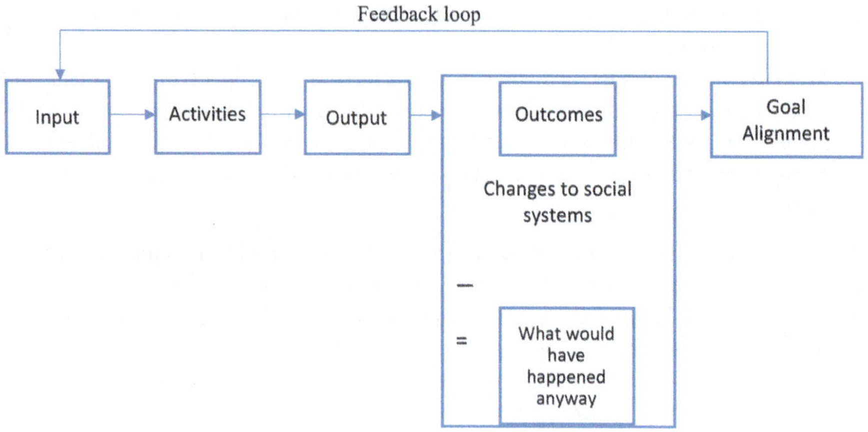

Fig. 2.9 Impact Value Chain—adapted from Clark et al. (2004); Maas and Liket (2011)

2.8 Assessing Impact Investment Practices: Tools, Frameworks and Databases

Despite the Impact Reporting and Investment Standards (IRIS) project providing a common set of definitions and terms for the field and, the Global Impact Investing Rating System (GIIRS), providing an analogue of the Standard and Poor's or Morningstar rating systems, using a common set of indicators to measure the social performance of funds and companies that intend to create impact, there are unsolved challenges—on why impact, what is impact, how and how much to measure, how to compare and aggregate impact (Lam & Tan, 2021) - and this is likely to affect the flow of funds into impact investing, and ultimately the development of the sector and the fulfilment of the UN SDGs. This stays true although according to the GIIRS the company's theory of change is already now embedded in each ratings report (GIIRS, 2012).

The questions has arised whether a unified framework (Lam & Tan, 2021) and a programme theory (Jackson, 2013) can help to harmonise and clarify what is measured, why and how, instead of looking just into harmonised reporting. One obvious challenge in investment (more than finance) is how the impact assessment and the progress measuring can be integrated into a valuation by the market (price building mechanism at the exchange) alternatively by introducing a special market segment with clear listing criteria. It is unclear currently whether this can help to bring about harmonisation, effective capital allocation, depth, width and resiliency, leaving valuation to a well established market, rather than to peer to peer matching platforms without a liquid market. The listing could happen based on clear listing criteria comparable ratings and reporting standards could develop - as usual in the asset management industry. An open question in this regard is, whether, taxonomies could help to pave the way to these harmonized listing criteria. Notably, GIIN initiated the first version of Impact Reporting and Investment Standards (IRIS) around 2009 with the intention of providing a universal language for social, environmental, and financial performance reporting. IRIS has since evolved into a catalog of performance metrics managed by GIIN. It is supposed to facilitate aggregation of performance data across diverse portfolios and improve investment comparability and performance benchmarking. The latest version, launched as IRIS + in 2019, exhibits efforts to increase user customisation and provides more defined concepts and structure for measuring impact according to the five dimensions they lay out. These are—identifying the outcomes to deliver, understanding baseline characteristics of stakeholders, understanding the degree of social changes, comparing performance with market benchmarks or control groups and lastly, understanding impact risks (Network, 2019c, 2019d).

At the level of individual investments, Rockefeller Philanthropy Advisors[4] has published a widely distributed handbook on how to design, implement and evaluate impact investments. Using a logic model that details the 'impact value chain' for a given investment, this guide distinguishes clearly between outputs (defined as the 'activity results', such as the number of people served by a project), on the one hand, and outcomes (defined as the collection 'of all results, intended and/or unintended', minus what would have happened anyway without the intervention). The authors of the handbook observe that 'most impact investors focus on the first order derivative output of their work (Jackson & Harji, 2012).

Further Lam and Tan (2021) provided an analysis based on secondary data in Asia on whether output, outcome or impact is measured by the current players in the field (Lam & Tan, 2021).[5] They reviewed a total of 44 impact investors and funds. Based on three characteristics of impact investing,

- Impact evaluation (which makes causal inferences on the results of an intervention through adequate control groups or baseline survey data),
- Outcome evaluation (which offer valid indicators to tests for change in social behavior or improved conditions) and
- Output reporting (which is akin to performance tracking of planned activities)

they found that it is unclear if these impact investors or funds use evidence-based impact data in designing their investments.{Lam & Tan, 2021) They refer to the International Finance Corporation IFC one of the first players in the field of impact investing (producing additionality). The IFC indicates that assessing the expected impact of each investment, based on a systematic approach is one of the principles of impact management; it is also vital for informing the investment design (IFC Corporation, 2019). However, such information is often not disclosed. The fund managers reviewed by Lam and Tan (2021) mostly claim to focus on creating social

[4]Rockefeller Philantropy Advisors (2012) Impact Investing Handbook: An Implementation Guide for Practitioners https://www.rockpa.org/project/new-impact-investing-handbook/.

[5]Subject to the limits of self-reporting, their list of impact investors is collated from the Asian Venture Philanthropy Network (AVPN) member list.

(and environmental) impact at scale, scalable impact or socially inclusive economic growth; some also mention their ESG goals and conscientiousness for responsible investments. All 44 publicly express their aim to achieve financial returns and social return on investment (Lam & Tan, 2021). They also looked into impact reporting based on 5 criteria: 1. eco-social goals based on the Sustainable Development Goals, 2. reporting publicly available, 3. reporting on outputs, 4.outcomes and 5.impact). Only 1 out of 44 fund managers fulfilled all five criteria, 6 fullfilled 4 criteria, another 5 fund managers fulfilled 3 criteria, meaning that all the rest 32 out of 44 were short in reporting about their mission and goals, and in particular about measurement of output, outcomes and impact. 24% of the sample (or ten out of 42 investors) reported on outcomes, or conducted assessments beyond outputs at the process level.

There is no shortage in impact design, management monitoring and reporting tools however, the following tools are available to the Impact Investor in accordance with (Clark et al., 2004; Maas & Liket, 2011; Lam & Tan, 2021) to evaluate the output, outcome and impact.

- Balanced Scorecard (BSc)
- Bottom of the Pyramid (BoP) Impact Assessment Framework
- Measuring Impact Framework (MIF)
- Millennium Development Goal Scan (MDG-scan)
- Ongoing Assessment of Social Impacts (OASIS)
- Participatory Impact Assessment
- Poverty and Social Impact Analysis (PSIA)
- Robin Hood Foundation Benefit–Cost Ratio
- Social Costs–Benefit Analysis (SCBA)
- Social e-Valuator
- Social Impact Assessment (SIA)
- Social Return on Investment (SROI)
- The IFC Performance Standards
- The International Standards for Sustainable Infrastructure (Sustainable Infrastructure Alliance)[6]
- Multilateral Development Banks' Harmonized Framework for Additionality in Private Sector Operations.

Despite this variety in frameworks in reality output, outcome and impact measurement appears to be still an important unresolved issue. There appears to be increasing efforts to develop new and more comprehensive tools of evaluation. While catalogues and summaries of measurement tools are helpful for practitioners looking for an appropriate way of conducting assessment, the problem remains that each method employs its own metrics and indicators. This would cause difficulty in making effectual cross references between results generated by different methods (Lam & Tan, 2021). This continues to be a hindrance for comparing performance of

[6] https://gib-foundation.org/wp-content/uploads/2020/05/International_Standards_for_Sustainable_Infrastructure-2.pdf April 2020.

impact funds and portfolios (Clark et al., 2004; Liket et al., 2014; Salazar et al., 2012; Schaltegger & Burritt, 2018) .

Also the variety of databases is compelling. Lam and Tan (2021) found databases with information that cannot be collapsed. The existing databases include B Impact Assessment by B Corp, Calvert Social Index, Charity Navigator, DJSI, Foundation Transparency Index, FSTE4Good, GiveWell, GRI, MSCI ESG, and UN Global Impact. They compared the databases comparing the following criteria, environment, social performance, financial performance, governance, qualifying assessment, ranking and type of asset considered. The table is displayed below in (Table 2.3).

The databases are not comparable by type of asset, scoring and some of them do not even allow a ranking of their constituents. This provides the investor and the impact designers finally with a very fragmented landscape. DJSI uses corporate sustainability scoring which may account for operational impact (in the sense of environment or governance in the ESG framework) but not necessarily the product impact in the sense of Brest and Born (2013). The DJSI also does not cater for all types of firms that would include charities and social enterprises beside the regular for-profit firms.

B Corp, on the other hand, covers all firm types, but it does not allow for comparability or aggregation across firm, firm types and over time. Moreover, there are databases, like Calvert, FSTE4Good, MSCI ESG and UN Global, which assess the ESG dimensions but exclude financial performance. This information corroborates the above mentioned challenge of defining, designing, measuring, managing and reporting impact. It is not clear that these frameworks are assessing impact in the sense that we adopt here as what impact is - any measurable and positive change in eco-societal outcomes that may be attributed to any intervention of a company (Lam & Tan, 2021).

In particular Jackson (2013) has recommended that at the level of the field as a whole, it is important to assess the perspectives and experience of industry leaders—asset owners, asset managers, demand-side actors and service providers—from both the Global North and Global South (Jacksonv2013). Open-ended qualitative interviews with leaders, as well as closed-ended surveys can be deployed (ibid).

2.9 Conclusions on Impact Investing and Its Problematic for Stock Exchanges

There is growing interest by investors for impact investing. We see a growing interest in co-creating eco-social impact, however investors now are waiting to understand what and how much impact their 502 bn USD invested into impact have produced. Despite a variety in frameworks in reality output, outcome and impact measurement are still an important unresolved issue. It is not clear that these frameworks are assessing impact in the sense that we adopt here as what

Table 2.3 Review of Existing Databases drawn form (Lam & Tan, 2021)

Name of databases	Environment	Social Performance	Govern-ance	Financial performance	Qualifying assessment	Ranking	Firm type
B Corp	X	X	X	X	X		All
Calvert	X	X	X		X		For-Profit
Charity Navigator			X	X	X	X	Charities
DJSI	X	X	X	X	X	X	For-Profit
Foundation Transparency Index		X	X	X		X	Public
FSTE4Good	X	X	X		X		All
GiveWell		X	X	X	X		Charities
GRI	X	X		X	X		All
MSCI ESG	X	X	X		X	X	Not-For-Profit
UN Global	X	X	X		X		All

impact is - any measurable and positive change in eco-societal outcomes that may be attributed to any intervention of a company (Lam & Tan, 2021, Brest and Born 2013).

The incompatibility of existing databases increases the issue of lack of transparency and consensus methodology forideating, creating, managing and measuring output, outcomes and impact of investments. Measuring impact according to the five dimensions they lay out.the five categories—identifying the outcomes to deliver ex ante, understanding baseline characteristics of stakeholders, understanding the degree of eco-social changes, comparing performance with market benchmarks or control groups and understanding impact risks are not yet established practice and clouded by the number of databases, tools, perspectives and definitions. Also the use of evidence-based impact data in designing investments is not taking place sufficiently. Cross-referencing and comparing results is currently likewise not possible as a unifying framework, clear criteria and a standard are absent. Creating such framework, consensus tools and standards would lead to a level playing field in impact investing, which could make it fit conventional investors requirements and tools.

2.10 Existing Product Structures with Impact Used at SSEs or in the Traditional Stock and Bonds Markets

The publication contributes to clarify the entire spectrum of impact investing instruments or lack thereof. I then tries to give a prognosis drawing form the knowledge obtained on under what conditions a Social Stock Exchange can contribute toimpact investing, whether and where such special platforms are needed and help. Understanding new concepts, instruments and dynamics thereby serving as guide for scholars and practitioners.

The author has already addressed the issue of lack of clarity in defining impact and impact investing. Academic literature show significant variations in the conceptualization of Impact Investing Care and Wendt (2018) and authors highlight that Impact Investing goes by many names (Hebb, 2013; Höchstädter & Scheck, 2015) including double and triple bottom line, mission related investing, program-related investment, blended-value, and economically targeted investing.

Also Höchstädter and Scheck (2015) investigates a large number of academic and practictioners works by highlighting several inconsistencies in definitional and terminological aspects. By analyzing only peer-reviewed work, Rizzello et al. (2016) depict the academic landscape of impact investing by providing a useful map of contributions, areas of inquiries and future research directions. However, despite these two works - Rizzello et al. (2016) and Höchstädter and Scheck (2015) - are two works that shed light on impact investing research area, but they do not provide an assessment of financial instruments and investment opportunities that are actually available in the impact investment market.

Thee is widespread agreement that impact investing is mobilizing capital for 'investments intended to create positive social impact beyond financial return'. Two key components of this definition are, first, the intent of the investor to achieve such impacts and that the investment has a double bottom line, considering aspects beyond financial returns.

Bugg-Levine & Emerson, 2011a, 2011b, p. 10) highlight that the idea behind impact investing is that investors can pursue financial returns while also intentionally addressing social and environmental challenges. Impact Investing definitions are based on two common principles: (1) the blended value principle and (2) the principle of sustainable financial return (Weber, 2016a, 2016b). In this sense, Weber (2016a, 2016b) clarify that these two principles distinguish impact investment from conventional investment because the latter is not striving for positive social impact but only for financial return (Weber, 2016a, 2016b, p. 86). However, the precise conceptual boundaries and terminology are still under discussion (Glänzel & Scheuerle, 2016), and other terms such as "social investment" (Dowling, 2017) are used to describe widely similar approaches. Some Authors uses the term "social impact investing" (Glänzel & Scheuerle, 2016; Chiappini, 2017).

There is little research on impact investing instruments. There is more to find on responsible and sustainable investment (see Meta-analysis provided by Clark et al., 2004). The term impact investment provide a broad rhetorical umbrella under which a wide range of investors could huddle (Bugg-Levine and Emerson, 2011a, 2011b, p. 12). Hummels & de Leede, (2014) defines microfinance as an exemplary case of impact investing. Grieco (2015) lists as example of impact investments Social impact bond, Developmental Impact Bond, Cash on delivery aid, Microfinance and Green Bond. Microfinance (Hummels & Millone, 2014), Private Equity, Venture Capital, Social Venture Capital, and Developmental Venture Capital are enclosed in the impact investing landscape by many authors (Martin, 2016). Impact Investors mainly use the following vehicles for activating impact investments. They set up Private Equity or Venture Capital Fund, use Direct Investment Strategies and to a lesser extend they have been experimenting with Social Bonds and Green Bonds. However the analysis from J.P. Morgan Social Finance and the GIIN network show that private equity is by far the most commonly used tool for impact investment.

The selection of asset classes shows - when putting it on an investment scale running from microfinance, seed, venture capital, private equity instruments are chosen that do not trade on a stock exchange. Secondary markets exist for venture capital and private equity, however the reasons for not making it to the secondary market are one of the areas the author was researching in the expert interviews.

As documented by Barman (2015), the early discussions about establishing a market for impact investing were very much focused on mobilizing investor demand. The goal was to link together distinct areas of investment such as clean technology, microfinance, and community development, under the general umbrella of impact investing, and introduce basic terminology and infrastructure that could steer the conversation and attract investor interest (see e.g. Monitor Institute, 2009a, 2009b). The previous history of practices such as social entrepreneurship, venture philanthropy, and SRI, had ensured that there were enough individuals and organizations predisposed to intuitively understand and internalize the basic idea behind impact investing. In short, a suitable set of cognitive instruments that determine how information about finance and investing is processed (Preda, 2005, 149) was in place and the initial efforts were quickly amplified into an 'impact investing movement' (Bugg-Levine, 2016).

In this chapter the authors analyses the contributions and embeddedness into finance markets of (1) social entrepreneurship and its funding and finance, (2) Green bonds (3) Social bonds and (4) project infrastructure bonds. The Big goals such as the Sustainable Development Goals require change at the systems level, and change-makers able to make this happen.this necessarily at the end of the day needs to produce new structures or the products developed have to fit into the market structure that exists. Key elements that help the leader and changemaker turn challenges into opportunities, create a vision, an action plan and a product, and make it actionable in the day-to-day are values, an adaptive decision making toolbox, frameworks and the mindset of entrepreneurship: (1) The personal values of the decision-maker form a key link between what drives the individual and the big goal. (2) Day-to-day decisions are informed by the personal value pyramid where these goals get practical, one decision at a time, and values help with fine-tuning. Current frameworks for decision making don't identify values as a key driver and neglect the role values play for sustaining the change-makers and for creating a movement and community necessary to make that change. As people evolve, so do their values to a more holistic, systemic way of being and doing, leading to better entrepreneurial decisions. (3) Entrepreneurship with its way of challenging assumptions, identifying needs and finding ways to address them and doing iterations until getting it right is the third key aspect how to make practical implementation possible of challenges that the social entrepreneur can solve using market mechanisms and how to gain traction.

2.11 Social Entrepreneurship and Social Economy Finance

The entrepreneurial space is particularly interesting as a seed bed, as this often is the forefront of change and innovation. Entrepreneurs as the primordial change-makers know this, the change they want to bring and the pain they want to alleviate is often intimately tied to their biography or their purpose. They could well be an even bigger force for good: Anchoring their bigger picture vision in the Sustainable Development Goals, linking this with their values and applying their business sense allows for new things to emerge that gain traction and scale up quicker to touch and transform more people's lives and to make a bigger and more positive impact. This includes both *what* entrepreneurs do but also *how* they are doing it. In the process, they also create meaningful livelihoods, grow leaders for future transformations and build clusters/tribes of likeminded individuals across the globe. This is how change accelerates.

A social entrepreneur takes an entrepreneurial risk to fulfill a social, ethical, or environmental world mission, using the method of entrepreneurship and the Journal for Social Entrepreneurship adds that these are organizations that do not see profit maximization as their primary business purpose, whether they set themselves up as a business, an NPO, or a government-sponsored organization.

So why are such social entrepreneurs relevant?

The number of jobs requiring social insurance is decreasing and more and more people are looking for meaningful employment. At the same time, technological progress is leading to rationalization and it is becoming increasingly important to maintain a human face in this so-called Economy 3.0. At the same time, after the financial crisis, the state had to withdraw from social programs in many countries or adopted cuts because the state funds were no longer sufficient. Social enterprises have stepped into this gap and filled it. They have thus taken on social concerns that were either not addressed or continued due to financial problems. This is how the third sector was created, which addresses social problems, creates jobs and meaning and contributes to the gross national product. Thus, the IBB - Investmentbank Berlin found out in a 2018 study: "Third sector companies generated an economic output of around 7 billion euros in Berlin in 2017. This corresponds to 5.8% of Berlin's total gross value added." In 2017, there were more than 470,000 social enterprises employing 1.44 million people in the UK alone. In France, social enterprises account for 10 percent of France's gross domestic product (GDP), 15% of Italy's GDP, and as much as 15.9% in the Netherlands and Belgium. The next generation in particular seems to be concerned about connecting business and society.

According to Deloitte's 2018 Human Capital Trends survey, organizations are increasingly being judged on the basis of their relationships with their employees, their customers and society, as well as their effects (impact) on society at large. This resulted in 77 percent of respondents rating citizenship and societal impact as a critical factor. Business is no longer just about making money adds Deloitte. Eighty-six percent of Millennials believe that business success should be measured by more than just financial performance. Apparently, we are becoming increasingly aware of our social responsibility. This is evidenced by the fact that well over half of all U.S. social enterprises were founded in 2006 or later. According to Social Change Central, more than 89% of social enterprises in India are less than 10 years old. In Canada, more than 57% of social enterprises were founded in the past 6 years. So it's fair to say that social enterprises are a new global trend. However, social enterprises have so far also been very individual in their business models. The question is how your models can scale, what strengthens scaling and what hinders it. After all, social impact is not primarily created by the innovative business model, but by the fact that the innovative business model is scalable and is scaled. Impact investors in particular place great value on this scalability, because it means that you can achieve more of the good, more social change, with more opportunities for returns at the same time. The challenge therefore lies in scaling the business model.

Nicholls, 2008 identifies 15 different challenges to social investment in his 2008 Skoll Center study. These fall into three categories of challenges: Unlocking investment from financial sources, developing sector-supportive infrastructure/policies, and improving the scalability of social enterprises to create greater absorptive capacity for financial capital.

1. for unlocking investment simultaneously from new and traditional sources, there is a lack of mechanisms to connect capital with entrepreneurs and providers of impact-driven investment opportunities. This is due in large part to an investment industry built on the historical binary of philanthropy (for impact and social impact) and investment (for returns), with each optimized independently. Bridging these two worlds does not occur and is further hindered by regulation. The binarity is reflected in regulation and legislation (Nicholls (2008).

   Therefore, the market for impact investing activities, lacks sufficient intermediaries or intermediaries- who connect the two concepts of doing good and doing well.
2. In addition, there is also a lack of market infrastructure, whether it is clearinghouses, syndicate facilities, independent third-party information sources, or investment advisors. Therefore, search and transaction costs for investors are high, with fragmented demand and supply, complex trades, and underdeveloped networks. Without an aggregation mechanism, investors have difficulty finding social enterprises that are sufficiently large to justify the fixed costs of conducting due diligence Nicholls (2008).
3. Nicholls (2008) cites the issue of scalability of business models as the third important category. He argues that the social enterprise sector suffers from a lack of sufficient absorptive capacity. This is best demonstrated, he says, by the limited number of companies with innovative, scalable models.

Based on interviews conducted by the Monitor Institute , 2008, the lack of sufficient absorptive capacity for capital is becoming an increasingly urgent challenge in the sector. Small social entrepreneurs cannot absorb enough capital, do not have a scalable business model that allows investors to invest in them. Funding trends in emerging markets suggest that absorptive capacity could become a significant bottleneck in the industry in the near future. It is already a challenge in markets such as India, where much capital is seeking deals (Monitor Institute (2008), Nicholls (2008)). Although the findings of Nicolls and the Monitor Institute have been around for over 10 years, these capital challenges have not changed much to date.

It remains the case to this day that investors want to invest large pools of capital, while the businesses of social entrepreneurs are relatively small.

This makes impact investing less attractive to investors. The scalability of the business model is therefore crucial for the success of social entrepreneurs with investors.

However, despite the challenges of the economic downturn, a number of opportunities have also emerged for investors in the social sectors.

An economic crisis like 2008, where financial exposure to conventional markets is accompanied by high volatility, drives investors into new sectors that are as uncorrelated as possible with the overall market. In other words, if the overall market falls, this has no impact on the uncorrelated sector. This is exactly the case with social entrepreneurs. Even in the economic crisis, they simply continue with their business model based on personal ethical convictions and did not experience a drop in profits. In addition, they have learned to manage without much external capital, they have to use their inner financial power generated from cash flow, bootstrap and further develop their business model from their own inner strength. This makes them very resilient to financial crises and thus represents a good "natural hedge" for investors. After all, it is obvious that in the countries where the economic crisis has hit the hardest, civil actions and social enterprise start-ups have increased the most, offering people a new perspective, both with their products and as employers. This resilience makes social enterprises in principle very attractive for investors, if they do two things: first - scale e.g. through social franchising and second - implement management systems. A recurring reproach from investors is that the entire decision-making structure of the social enterprise is designed around the founder and that management systems common in normal business are missing. If social entrepreneurs can solve these two issues, they are a decisive step further. The independence or resilience or uncorrelatedness to the financial markets is at the same time an opportunity for social enterprises. Investors' desire for diversification, resilience, and uncorrelatedness of investment with what is happening in the capital markets has led investors to look at sectors such as microfinance that tend to be less correlated with the broader market (Kraussa & Walter, 2008).

4. Does Know-How Transfer Take Place or is Each Social Entrepreneur Unique?

It is quite surprising that despite the desire to be uncorrelated with the capital markets, more capital is not flowing to social entrepreneurs, which the author believes has to do with the lack of scaling of the business model to date. Social entrepreneurs are often in a precarious position. They are supposed to be the "rain maker," making the impossible possible.... "A social entrepreneur is expected to bear the normal startup risks, be highly innovative, solve a social problem, report every two months to foundations that support them - all for a pittance." Focusing on the founder is the undoing of many social entrepreneurs. It fails to recognize the team effort and prevents the social entrepreneur from transferring know-how to other members of society. Here, once again, the lack of tools and management systems becomes apparent. This lack exists not only for risk and efficiency evaluation, but also for questions like- organizes and orchestrates an own ecosystem, in which the roles of the social entrepreneurs complement each other and a large business field emerges from the small social enterprise. For any large company, knowledge transfer is a very important issue. If the knowledge carriers leave the company, the company must still have access to the knowledge developed by them in their function. However, the tools of knowledge transfer are still too little used in social enterprises and finally the lack of knowledge - and know how transfer prevents the scaling and thus the further growth. This, in turn, then leads investors to view the company as not sufficiently capital-absorbing and also to doubt the "investment readiness" of the social enterprise. If no knowledge transfer takes place, the impact remains low, because the possibilities for scaling are not sufficiently exploited.

5. How can knowledge transfer take place in the social enterprise?

It is important to understand that in social enterprises there are different types of knowledge (know how, know what and know why) which are not easily transferable due to their complex, implicit and highly personal nature. Knowledge transfer is considered a focused activity that promotes the exchange of ideas, experiences, skills, and lessons learned to support and influence decision making and problem solving. Transfer activity occurs at two primary levels:

Group level - The knowledge resides in its organizational members, tools, tasks, networks, and external communities. By sharing this knowledge and experience, this group can achieve its objectives or.

Individual level - Often the knowledge remains tacitly with individuals because the knowledge dimensions are difficult to articulate and often occur as a result of learning processes.

The main goal of a knowledge transfer is to enable others to benefit from these personal experiences, to make the tacit knowledge explicit, to put it down in management systems to enable others to make better decisions and find better ways to solve problems.

Knowledge is often further differentiated. A distinction is made between knowledge about data and facts (know-how) and so-called experience and process knowledge (expertise). Contact or access to specific people is sometimes considered a separate form of knowledge (know-who).

Key factors that would indicate successful knowledge transfer are the absorption and application of knowledge. This involves both a cognitive understanding of the knowledge transferred/shared (absorption) and the ability to apply that knowledge in context. (Application). Many of the same principles, practices, and methods (storytelling, interviewing, shadowing) for knowledge transfer found in commercial settings can also be applied in social settings. This would already increase absorption.

6. What are the possibilities for a social enterprise to scale?

It needs structured management methods that play on issues such as product development, development of its own market (market development), so that the application of knowledge in the context can spread quickly and the product can scale. At the same time, the scaling strategies depend on the key factors of the social enterprise and the ability of the enterprise to scale and under which model must be thoroughly studied in this regard. Basic requirements are viability of the operational model and the necessary management competencies, which are best reflected in management systems as well. And here lies the crux: social enterprises are often in a single location and would actually need management systems to scale their business model, which they have been able to do without due to their manageable size. The business model must be replicable. Replicability of the company's operating model is the core aspect of any attempt at scale.

Reproducibility is understood here as the ability of an organization to replicate not only its products and services but also, where appropriate, its structures and processes - nationally and internationally (Alter, 2007; Dees et al., 2004; Winter & Szulanski, 2001). The more an operational model can be simplified and reduced to its core pillars-for example, through standardization and mechanization-the greater the chances that these components can be replicated later. Core components are those that generate social impact most effectively. In the Bertelsmann Stiftung's experience, the easiest way to identify such components is to use an "elevator pitch." Three sentences that could be used when ridden in an elevator for 60 seconds to explain why the operating model is unique. In addition, commercially successful companies have shown that standardization and, when possible, the development of IT-based solutions can facilitate and simplify the development of scaling processes (Von Krogh & Cusumano, 2001). It is then also a question of whether the founders/managers alone will be able to generate the various resources that the social enterprise will need at the different stages of the scaling process, or alternatively, whether they will be able to mobilize these resources from third parties or through their own social network, i.e., by using their own social capital. And here it appears that social enterprises are so stretched that the establishment of an ecosystem that would enable the use of their own social capital has been omitted. The resources needed are mainly financial capital, human resources - especially knowledge - and other social contacts that may provide access to additional resources or partners. Any attempt to scale ultimately means mobilizing internally or externally. Raising resources under difficult conditions is a major challenge for new and small social enterprises, as any commercial startup wants to grow. To make it even more difficult, unlike commercial enterprises, social enterprises often cannot pay competitive market prices for staff, financing, and other factors of production, primarily because they do not claim market prices themselves. These enterprises must find other means to secure the resources they need, particularly in the areas of financing, knowledge, and human resources (Austin et al., 2006).

"Effect" - Growth and Impact in Civil Society," is a joint project of the Bertelsmann Stiftung and the Association of German Foundations. The project has systematically gathered scientifically sound knowledge and practical experience on scaling social business models. The scientific analysis was conducted by Professor Christiana Weber of the Institute of Management and Organizational Behavior at Leibniz University in Hanover, who had already developed the first international framework for assessing the scalability of social impact for the World Bank in 2011.

In 2013, the scaling strategies of 24 socially motivated organizations were analyzed based on existing research. The results were published in the Scaling Social Impact Handbook. One thing up front. The best strategy cannot help if the necessary success factors - inside or outside the organization - are not sufficiently in place. The focus of both scaling for social enterprises must therefore be on the connection between success factors and scaling strategy. The different combinations of success factors, strategy and overall success among the European social enterprises surveyed in the Bertelsmann study also confirm the so-called configuration approach, according to which certain organizational combinations, forms or "archetypes" are more successful than others and therefore scale more frequently (Mintzberg, 1980/1989).

Here one can distinguish four strategy types, always provided that the social enterprise has a viable operating model is both financially viable and has generated demonstrable social impact. The 4 strategy types can be explained as follows (see Dees et al., 2004; CASE, 2003, , 2006; Weber, 2012):

1. capacity building: Social programs are scaled up from an existing region, either through government support, social franchising in the region.
2. strategic expansion: new sites are established, new products / services are introduced.

   New audiences are targeted and / or geographic expansion is accelerated.
3. contract partnerships: New locations are established in long-term cooperation with contractual partners. The associated loss of control by the founder is often an obstacle, although this would be the right way to scale the product.
4. dissemination of knowledge: The concept / operating model of the social enterprise is shared without expanding the organization itself. This can be represented in licensing models.

Given the recent upsurge in social entrepreneurship, impact driven business models and a broad policy push by the Paris Climate Accord, the UN Sustainable Development goals, the Agenda 2030 and recently the EU Action plan for financing sustainable growth there should also be no shortage of investors and financiers eager to absorb this demand. However the shortcoming mentioned above in social entrepreneurial ecosystems hinder the scalability of the makret. Stock exchanges are the market places for trading financial instruments. It is the place where investees can raise capital in the secondary market through an Independent Public Offering (IPO) or an Independent Coin Offeirng (ICO), when the asset has been tokenized. It is also the place where investor demand and impact offer meet. The problem, as emphasized both by WEF lies in matching assets that create positive impact with investors in a manner that is efficient, effective, transparent, and scalable (WEF 2013). However when it comes to the institutional investor and impact funds, institutional investors fear nothing more than a deterioration in asset quality. Like in microfinance social entrepreneurship has to address the issue of asset quality. How can the market grow without encouraging worse assets to enter the market place and the SSE. Some of the recommendations above, when social entrepreneurs and sSSEs adopt an ecosystem approach may help in addressing these issues.

In addition to investment vehicles, the author has researched the investee side of impact investing. In particular microfinance, social entrepreneurship, green and clean tech as well as healthtech are targets of impact investors. Social entrepreneurship is considered to provide impact in its purest terms. The term "social entrepreneur" has more recently been described as those who establish businesses primarily to meet a social aim rather than for personal pecuniary benefit. Research that does exist primarily focuses on the characteristics of the social entrepreneur and their motivation to establish a social enterprise (e.g. Germak & Robinson, 2014; Smith et al., 2013; Lehner & Germak, 2014; Korsgaard, 2011; Christopoulos & Vogl, 2015) with little understanding of the contemporary practice, opportunities and challenges encountered by social entrepreneurs. Social entrepreneurs have been described as value-orientated individuals who create social change through the start up of an enterprise (Certo & Miller, 2008), as innovators who achieve social change through enterprise (Zahra et al. 2008), and as individuals who are motivated by the opportunity to adopt an innovative approach to pull together resources and networks to satisfy needs which the state cannot or fails to provide (Thompson et al., 2000). While there is no definitional consensus, the focus on social value is consistent across various definitions (Peredo & McLean, 2006; Shaw & Carter, 2007) as well as an understanding that the characteristics of social entrepreneurs, the opportunities they pursue, and the outcomes of their businesses diverge somewhat from typical business approaches (Mair & Noboa, 2006). Rather than solely relying on charitable donations and/or grant funding, social enterprises may seek to use trading activities to achieve social goals and financial sustainability (Sacchetti & Campbell, 2014). Certo and Miller (2008) suggest that to achieve growth and/or to ensure sustainability social entrepreneurs must develop their business and manage resources with a commercial as well as social mission. Robinson (2006) argues that whilst the decision of commercial entrepreneurs to pursue entrepreneurial activities depends largely on the extent of economic barriers, social entrepreneurs face challenges related to both social and institutional structures. To counteract these challenges, the use of networks has been found to be important for social entrepreneurs and enterprises in acquiring resources, reaching customers, identifying opportunities and generating support from the local community (Sacchetti & Campbell, 2014; Hynes, 2009; Shaw & Carter, 2007). A survey conducted by Christopoulos (2019) suggests that In terms of challenges associated with the achievement of success of the social enterprises, narrative responses fell into several themes. First, lack of funds available was mentioned by more than 50% of respondents directly. A further half referred to a lack of staff. Cumulatively, these responses suggested a lack of resources as a challenge for the social enterprise.

The creation of SSEs, an "expensive and long-term market building venture," (OECD, 2014, p. 21) represents an important aspect of this more general process of discursive and institutional development.

J.P. Morgan Social Finance and GIIN further examine and explore impact investment dynamics in several publications, such as in "Perspectives on Progress: the Impact Investor Survey" (GIIN, 2012).

The report reveals the experiences, expectations, and perceptions of 99 impact investors in 2012, and their plans for 2013. Investors surveyed for the report include fund managers, development finance institutions, foundations, diversified financial institutions, and other investors with at least USD ten million committed to impact investment. Respondents also reported the instruments that they use to make impact investments. Unsurprisingly, most of the respondents state using venture capital and private equity, so alternative assets that exist outside of the stock and bond markets.

These assets however could be found on SSE s that do a direct investee investor matching. Private equity and venture capital however are assets that are not liquid or fungable so it is hard for the investor to exit the deal other than after some years through an Initial public offering, a sell. Off or a merger and acquisition. Currently there are no figures available how high or low the survivor bias is, meaning how many assets and social entrepreneurship models have survived and how many failed. The private equity market and the venture capital market which social entrepreneurs are using today may profit from an increased visibility of the social impact asset through the listing on the SSE, and as all private equity and venture capital assets it may enjoy an uncorrelated beta, so no impact on th asset when there is an impact on the stock market. The multiples earned with such assets are also unknown, so we can state that for SSEs the argument of additional value for the social entrepreneur through the listing process and higher salience may apply, however the questions of liquidity, transferability, survivor bias, impact definition, assessment and reporting, measurability of impact and quantification of impact all remain unsolved. The market resembles more complete black box, where SSEs can claim the benefit of making social impact assets more salient and—at least for this one SSE more comparable to other private equity and venture capital impact assets.

Private equity is one investment approach within impact investing. It employs the traditional private equity model that intends to generate an attractive financial return for fund managers and their investors. The private equity process is one in which investors structure an investment vehicle (private equity fund) to raise capital from major institutional and individual investors (such as pension funds, endowments and high net worth individuals), committing the commingled capital into private businesses to expand and improve their operations, and ultimately, and usually after several years, to sell their stake in these businesses or to take them public on a stock exchange in many cases as an Independent Public Offering (IPO).

An important attribute of private equity is that it can enable access to vast pools of financing through global capital markets. By comparison, funding sources such as government aid and philanthropic finance are often limited (and unpredictable) in low-income countries, and represent only a fraction of what is potentially available from the capital markets. Funding from Development Finance Institutions (DFI) may be significant in scale and can play a catalytic role, but is usually only available on the condition that additional private equity and therefore raise much more money than with crowd funding for instance. In addition it will impose much more restrictions on impact investors and normally is bound to a proven track record, which may not exist in the infancy stage in which many impact investment businesses find themselves.

For example, equity investment can be a more favourable capital base than debt for the many businesses with potential impact that are testing new business models to deliver products or services to consumers who have inconsistent and low incomes. "Some new business models require significant customer education, which can be capital intensive and can take some time to translate into revenues, which can make it challenging to service a debt investment", explained Yasemin Saltuk of J.P. Morgan Social Finance. In certain situations, particularly in frontier markets or early stage businesses, portfolio companies can face volatile cash flows, unpredictable supply chains, poor infrastructure, or inefficient regulation. This can translate into volatile cash flows for the businesses, making debt payments a burden, especially at high interest rates. As private equity and venture capital are fit for providing its investors with exit strategies like Independent Public Offering and Independent Coin Offerings, one has to wonder, why impact investors have not used secondary markets so far to make impact investing both accessible to the normal investor and scaling exponentially. One could argue fresh money for the impact investees scales the impact company. The real effect of impact investing may therefore not lie in investing in impact, but in scaling the impact. Therefore the author is investigating why impact investment are not brought to secondary markets and to what extent this hampers the development of impact investing, as the impact can be multiplies through scaling and fast growth. In other words the real impact may lie in scaling the impact. Rather than in kick start financing the impact.

Attracting institutional capital remains a significant constraint to the development of impact investing. Although increasing in size and prominence in the past several years, private equity-style impact investing remains a "niche" investment strategy according to Bridges Ventures that mainstream institutional investors do not typically include in their portfolios. Attracting institutional investors will require evidence that it is possible to achieve both impact and financial returns, and education of investors about appropriate opportunities in which to invest. For instance, "FIR Capital" has raised awareness locally in Brazil by convening private wealth managers, the Brazilian private equity association, universities, pension funds and journalists, with the support of the Brazilian private equity association ABVCAP (EMPEA).

2.12 Green Bonds

The idea of issuing bonds dedicated to fund projects with positive environmental impact is about a decade old. The first green bond was issued by the European Investment Bank in 2007, with the World Bank following suit. Until 2012, the green bond market was a few billions of dollars niche filled by multilateral development banks. Then, different kinds of issuers started to pick up the idea resulting in green bonds issued also by municipals, merchant banks and corporates, and such ones constructed as ABS as well. The emerging market obviously lacked clarity to the definitions and processes associated with green bonds. This was why a group of banks initiated the development of the Green Bond Principles (GBP) which were first released January 2014. At the same time, the green bond market powerfully accelerated with a total issuance of about 35 billion USD in 2014. Currently, the total issuance of labelled green bonds sums up to about 150 billion USD.

Measuring the issuance of green bonds has led to ambiguous results. This is because no mechanism existed which would distinguish whether a bond is a green one. The Green Bond Principles, being the most important reference for green bonds, label itself as 'voluntary process guidelines'. They not only lacked the power to impede misuse but also fell short from defining a minimum standard. While the 'use of proceeds' rather clearly demands that the utilization of the proceeds should provide clear environmental benefits, the other principles remained vague. This changed when ICMA the International Capital Market Association entered the space and created its green bond standard, requiring minimum principles for green bonds. Concerning the Process for Project Evaluation and Selection and the Management of Proceeds, the GBP 'encourage a high level of transparency'; for the reporting, a framework is provided (GBP 2016, p. 4). The recommendation of an external review, known as SPO (Second Party Opinion), originally has not been one of the principles. While confining itself to a recommendation framework is normal for a voluntary agreement, market participants have been confronted with limited transparency. Accordingly, any issuing institution could not be prevented from labelling its bond as a green bond even if an analysis would find a negative net sustainability impact of the bond. This has changed now the U Green Bond, which is part of the EU Action Plan. The clarity the regulation now provides has kicked of a record increase in green bonds.

The Climate Bonds Initiative has reported another record increase in 2021 (Climate Bonds Initiative 2021).

According to the climate Bonds initiative the approach to COP26 entails a reimagination of the future for stakeholders across all sectors and nations. This defining moment in climate history has given fresh impetus to sustainable debt markets with Q3 of 2021 witnessing a new record annual figure for labelled debt, months before the year's end.

The climate Bonds initative highlights the following Key Factors

- Combined labelled issuance of Green, Social, and Sustainability, Transition, and Sustainability-linked reached **USD767.5bn** in the first three quarters of 2021,
- September 2021—was the largest issuing month ever, **USD130.6bn** of total labelled issuance
- Cumulative total labelled issuance stood at **USD2.3tn** at end Q3 2021; cumulative green at USD **1.2tn**
- Green bonds reach USD 354.2bn at end Q3 2021, surpassing 2020 total and now likely to reach half a trillion by year end of 2021
- Sustainability-linked bonds reach USD78.7bn this year; transition finance reaches USD5bn this year.

All in labelled and thematic bonds therefore now enjoy a market share of around 3 percent of the total bond market.

In recent years, green bonds have become the rising stars of the global bond markets not only for those who are interested into sustainable finance. Despite the fact that the market share of green bonds is still well beyond 1%, the public showed strong interest into this kind of financial instrument supposed to be the answer of the financial industry to the global ecological challenges, especially to the climate change. The kind of innovation linked to the green bonds is remarkable: On the one hand, they are formally just straightforward bonds so investors happen to buy one without taking notice of the fact. On the other hand, green bonds make use of innovative concepts such as transparency requirements or the decoupling of recourse scope and the proceeds which are earmarked for green projects. What is more, only a fuzzy definition exists which bond may be labelled as a 'green' one.

s leads to ambiguous results. This is because no mechanism exists which would distinguish whether a bond is a green one. The Green Bond Principles, being the most important reference for green bonds, label itself as 'voluntary process guidelines'. They not only lack the power to impede misuse but also fall short from defining a minimum standard. While the 'use of proceeds' rather clearly demands that the utilization of the proceeds should provide clear environmental benefits, the three other principles remain vague. Concerning the Process for Project Evaluation and Selection and the Management of Proceeds, the GBP 'encourage a high level of transparency'; for the reporting, a framework is provided (GBP 2016, p. 4). The recommendation of an external review, known as SPO (Second Party Opinion), is not one of the four principles. While confining itself to a recommendation framework is normal for a voluntary agreement, market participants are confronted with limited transparency. Accordingly, any issuing institution cannot be prevented from labelling its bond as a green bond even if an analysis would find a negative net sustainability impact of the bond.

The charme of green bonds is that they do at least require proceeds to be invested into a climate neutral investment. While this does not change the underlying that provided the proceeds it has a positive impact on the investment of the proceeds in the future and instills the search for green assets. As it is structured like a normal bond, just with an escrow account, where the proceeds for the green investment are parked it is compatible with existing financial markets. While it does not qualify as a clear impact investment, it has some ex ante and forward looking elements for investing the earmarked escrow amount into green assets. This has been just a promise prior to the development of principles and now the EU Green Bond which has boosted the market.

Conclusions and Learning When Contrasting Green Bonds to Impact Assets

The Green Bond therefore is a good example that when the structuring has been done right an impact like product with a forward looking mechanism and a blended value approach (with a strategic product element to be invested into green technology) can meet the traditional bond market demand. The difference between the SSEs, social enterprise finance and funding of green assets though private capital or SSEs is that the green bond was invented by the Capital Markets themselves it added just a thematic element to the plain vanilla well known bond structure, often in a way (in defining use of proceeds in the underlying contract) that the market participant was even not aware of the additional gimmick. Being very loose in its requirements in the beginning, regulators like the French Government and later the EU have tightened conditions and created a uniform framework and set of conditions by further developing a voluntary standard. Figure 2.10 illustrates how the EU has used the existing ICMA framework to come up with its EU Green Bond Scheme that created a great deal of clarity for institutional investors what the EU regards as minimum standard for a Green bond in the EU (in coordination with the European Securities and Markets Association ESMA). As can be concluded from Fig. 2.10 the EU Green Bond has strengthened the use of proceeds definition, the eligibility criteria tor a EU Green bond through the publication of the Green Bond Framework, defining clear Green Bond Management and Reporting Criteria to what green projects the escrow funds have been allocated and the mandatory external verification. Other than with assets traded on an SSE, the institutional market has created a loose quasi green product that could be introduced easily on the market even in the beginning it was mainly greenwash and was entirely compatible, leading to an upgrade and standardization by regulators thereafter. In contrast to the SSEs, that have been developed by Social entrepreneurs, foundations, private impact investors and their networks like GIIN, but not the financial institutional markets the light green bond was compatible to the market and now left the status of a greenwash bond thanks to the regulation of the EU Action Plan that has based on the then existing voluntary principles. Therefore on SSEs the structure of the investor, the investee and the existing assets ad products follow much more a black box idiosyncratic model where clear criteria for valuation of an asset are missing and SSEs only partially address the transparency issues.

Figure 2.10 illustrates the EU Green Bond Mechanis.

In contrast to the SSEs, that have been developed by Social entrepreneurs, foundations, private impact investors and their networks like GIIN, but not the financial institutional markets the SSEs has different structures from the kind of investor, the investee and last but not least the existing assets ad products follow much more a black box idiosyncratic model where clear criteria for valuation of an asset are missing and SSEs only partially address the transparency issues. The products themselves are designed with the focus on idiosyncratic design and the focus has never been finding a product that will be compatible with financial markets. This has led to all kinds of inconsistencies, in defining impact, in creating assessment and investors are left in the dark about survival rates, survival bias, tracking error against an alternative investment which would be investing in an alternative assets impact fund and the traceability in risk adjusted performance of that alternative impact fund in comparison to an SRI fund according to the EU SFDR regulation. Instead the private investors prefer the idiosyncratic black box alternative investment approach as they want to have a uncorrelated beta to the financial markets and not be transparent about their valuation criteria, principles and multiples. At the same token however, this black box approach leaves the institutional investor out, who has fiduciary duties and therefore has to justify investment based on a proven back-tested risk adjusted return perspective. In the case of impact investments, the institutional investor would likewise have to justify how he has defined, managed

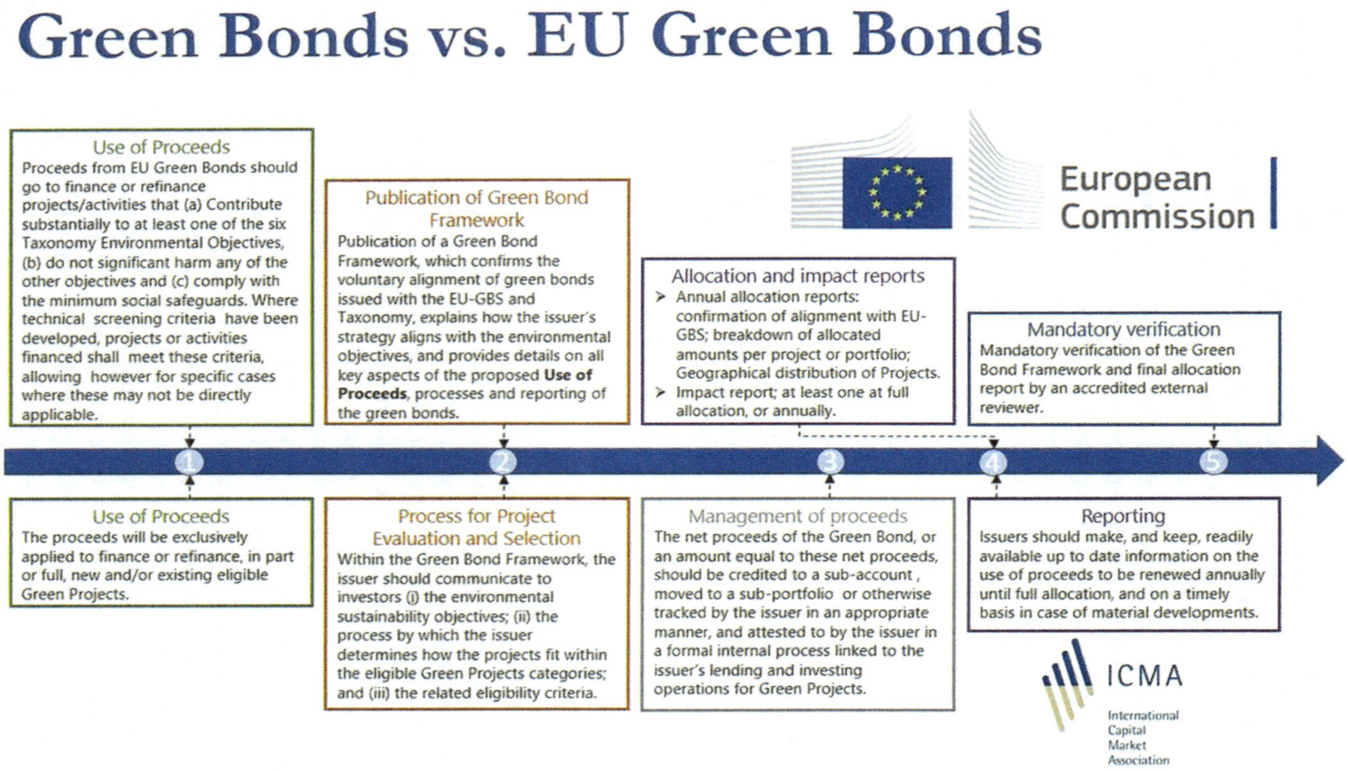

Fig. 2.10 The EU Green Bond versus the Green Bond

and controlled impact, which is impossible without having quantifiable indicators. So the lack of quantifiable impact measurement, the idiosyncratic black box approach in valuations, the intransparent model precludes institutional investors from investing into impact assets. In addition the small lot size and lack of fungibility does not really help the market to scale.

2.13 Social Impact Bonds

Social & Sustainability bonds comprised just over a third (31.1%) of total labelled issuance in Q3 2021 (USD74.2bn), bringing cumulative Social & Sustainability issuance to USD 981.1bn. After a record breaking 2020 in which Q1 exceeded 2019 total issuance, Q3 2021 saw the market stabilise post-pandemic.

A Social bond structure normally includes a pay for performance Scheme. A societal issue like youth unemployment or criminality recidivism rates that cost the public sector money are handed over to a private entity with the goal to reduce significantly the youth unemployment or recidivism rate. A reduction level is defined. The private partner will receive a performance payment if the private partner is able to achieve the reduction rate or even outperform it. The performance obligation can be structured in form of a scoail bond (Fig. 2.11).

The social bond is a twitter that has been designed in way that is already compatible with market structures and can be issued like a normal bond. The social

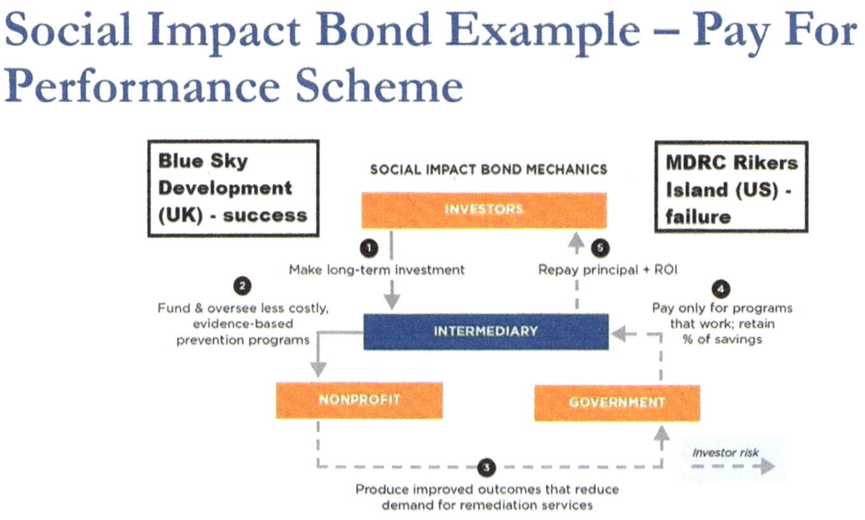

Fig. 2.11 Social Impact Bond

bond therefore does not need any platform or SSE scheme, it enter the traditional financial market with an underlying the fulfils the promise of social entrepreneurship. The social problem is solved using market mechanisms and in this case the market mechanism is clearly set up by the pay for performance scheme. Only when the decrease of the negative societal effect has been reduced by the defined percentage in the contract, the private partner (social entrepreneur) receives the performance payment. There is still an under researched area on whether institutional investors can participate in the market due to lot size and also a comparison between risk adjusted returns of an SRI fund and a social bond is still unavailable. One could argue that an SRI Fund is ESG driven and based on market indices, however the professional investor needs to know, what extra return he gets for the impact materialization risk he is taking (if reduction not achieved no performance payment) when buying a social bond. He also needs to know the tracking error of a social bond portfolio to the an SRI fund in order to determine how much return he gets for his impact risk.

Another area where positive and negative impacts are created, mitigated managed and measured is the Project finance and Infrastructure bond industry bond industry, where infrastructure funds are created and invested in by pension funds and investment banks. These transaction most of the time follow a public private partnership scheme as detailed in Fig. 2.12. Whereas project bonds normally have positive and negative (mitigated impacts and a clear impact assessment and impact management structure they are to be counted into the sphere of blended value, as they are not designed to solve a societal problem primarily, but have for sik evaluation the impact assessment and impact positive opportunities screening process in place. If one defined green bonds and project bonds as impact bonds the scaling of the market would look much roier, however these two forms do not sufficient to solve the positive impact asset creation problem explained in the social entrepreneurship section and impact sections of this document. The overarching market appetite can

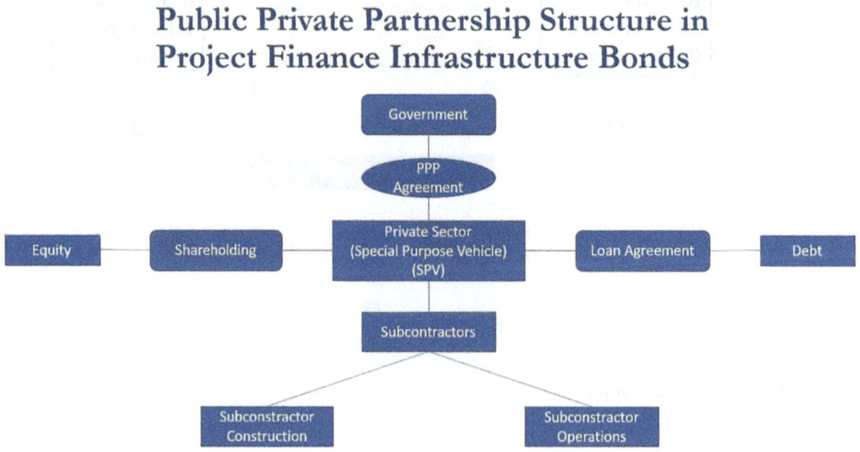

Fig. 2.12 Public Private Partnership Scheme in Project finance

be seen by the fact that both Green Bonds and Project Bonds are immediately over-subscribed by professional market participants as soon as they come to market and normally carry therefore a considerable premium which cannot be justified by additional assessment and management costs (for green bond the premium is currently around seven basis points). So the market could digest much more of these valuable products, which again follow a blended value perspective rather than a strict impact perspective.

Chapter 3
Traditional Stock Exchanges

3.1 Functions of Stock Exchanges

According to Michie one of the primary functions of a stock exchange is to provide a quick, persistent and constant demand for purchase and sale of security and to establish a liquid market (Michie 1987). In details the functions can be categorized as follows according to Michie (ibid).

- Providing Liquidity and Marketability to Existing Securities—It gives the chance to investors to disinvest and reinvest.
- Pricing of Securities—Stock Exchanges fix prices for shares trading on it. Share prices are determined by the forces of demand and supply.
- Stock exchanges guarantee safety of transactions—existing legal framework provides, which are operated through the stock exchange provide a safe and fair deal in securities market.
- Contribute to economic growth—through the process of disinvestment and reinvestment, savings will turn into investment avenues. This leads to capital formation and economic growth.
- Spreading of an equity cult—stock exchanges encourage people to save and invest in securities.
- Providing scope for speculation—stock Exchange gives scope for speculation within the limits of the law. Stock Exchange encourages the speculative activity in a restricted and controlled manner.
- Stock exchange improves the company's performance through the regulated reporting.
- Stock exchanges help in raising new capital—The new companies and existing companies need capital for their activities. The Stock Exchanges are helpful in raising capital both by new and old companies.

In short liquidity is a precondition to enable constant sale and purchase of securities and a smooth price building mechanism. This plus the regulation differentiates them

K. Wendt, *Social Stock Exchanges*, Sustainable Finance,
https://doi.org/10.1007/978-3-030-99720-5_3

from platforms. The NASDAQ explains liquidity in its glossary of financial terms as the ease with which securities can be bought and sold without wide price fluctuations.

3.2 Comparing Traditional Markets Key Determinants with the SSEs

First of all it is relevant to know which determinants of a market place the SSEs currently fulfill. For institutional investors that must be able to trade so assets liquidity is a key criterion. Liquidity is measured by four dimensions: market depth and width, immediacy and resiliency (Osterhelweg and Schiereck 1993).

Market depth includes the presence of sufficiently limited buy and sell orders to execute new orders without major price movements. It refers to the number of shares offered or demanded at the respective bid-ask spread.

This allows a deep market. In a deep market the number of shares that are quoted at the market spread or a price close to the market spread is high and existing temporary imbalances between buy and sell orders are balanced by orders available in the market without large price jumps.

A liquid market also fulfils the dimension of **breadth (width)** of a market meaning that limited buy and sell orders reach volume to execute larger orders without a strong price effects. This entails the inclusion of a market maker function. In Market Maker Markets the market maker quotes bid-ask spreads for a given number of securities to ensure the liquidity of the market. The market measure for breadth (width) is the closeness of the best bid and ask prices to each other, i.e. the closer the bid and ask prices are to each other, the lower the cost per security traded.

As liquidity is also defined by the ability to convert an asset into cash equal to its current market value, the dimensions of **immediacy and resiliency (renewal power)** come into play.

Immediacy can be described as the time required to execute a transaction of a certain size. The shorter the time lag between the decision to execute a transaction and the ability to execute that transaction on desired terms, the higher the level of immediacy offered by a market. In market maker markets the market makers are permanently available during trading hours to fulfill customer orders.

Renewal power (resiliency) determines how quickly prices return to their starting point after deviating from the equilibrium price due to large order imbalances that are not due to the presence of new information.

In a market with high renewal power counter orders eliminate the imbalance in the case of short-term order imbalances, immediately and flow into the market.

Platforms called ISX or SSX currently do not have any market making, are short in liquidity so they are missing breath and width, immediacy and renewal power and as a consequence liquidity, if an impact investor wants to sell he has to find a direct match. The 502 bn USD invested are spread over a number of platforms and to a large extent deals done without any platform at all. A market lacking liquidity cannot fulfil the four key dimensions of depth, breath, immediacy and renewal power. The criteria of transparency are only partially fulfilled as different definitions of impact investing are used, so the platforms are not harmonized in their approach. Transaction speed when done through direct matching will be sufficient for investors demands, there is no analysis available yet for transaction security and information efficiency. The research from Lam and Tan (2021) showing incomplete submissions to the transaction platform, missing data on impact and impact assessments suggests that we cannot assume information efficiency as of an information efficient market arbitrage should be possible (at least between the different SSEs, which is not the case due to different design and different approaches, different information requirements). Another prerequisite for information efficiency is that all information is available at the same time and all places. This appears not to be the case when information on important impact data is missing. The direct matching approach and the valuations hided in a black box do not create transparency. A comparison with other assets traded on stock or bond markets is not possible. So there is no transparency on whether the valuations on the transaction platforms are trading at market value and to what valuation criteria and approaches they could be compared to. As the platforms constitute a direct market matching between investees and investors the valuations are negotiable and finally not transparent, in addition based on incomplete transaction information. The lack of liquidity as a consequence of absence of breath, width, renewal power and immediacy, and the lack of transparency and information efficiency have a compound negative effect on these platforms, which cannot been compared to traditional stock exchanges with their key functions. They may be able when they further develop to allow for a double blind auction process, but such auction process would at least require transparency and information efficiency. Therefore one question arising is whether impact investing needs a liquid stock exchange to grow and whether the current ISX/SSX have to be redesigned and how such redesign should look like (Fig. 3.1).

3.3 Blueprinting Social Stock Exchanges

As documented by Barman (2015), the early discussions about establishing a market for impact investing were very much focused on mobilizing investor demand. The goal was to link together distinct areas of investment such as clean technology, microfinance, and community development, under the general umbrella of impact investing, and introduce basic terminology and infrastructure that could steer the conversation and attract investor interest (see e.g. Monitor Institute 2009a, b). The previous history of practices such as social entrepreneurship, venture philanthropy, and socially responsible investing (SRI), had ensured that there were enough individuals and organizations predisposed to intuitively understand and internalize the basic idea behind impact investing. In short, a suitable set of cognitive instruments that determine how information about finance and investing is processed

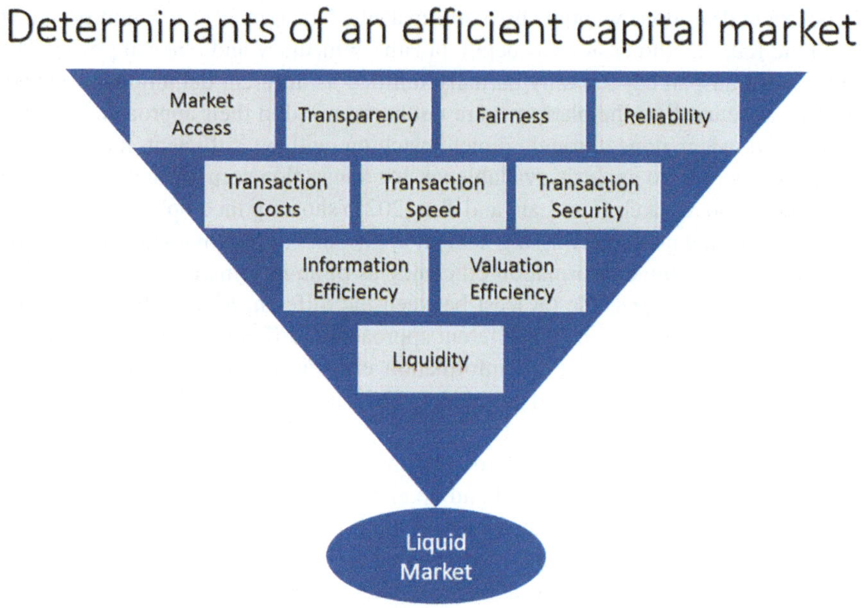

Fig. 3.1 The structure and variables

(Preda 2005, p. 149) was in place and the initial efforts were quickly amplified into an 'impact investing movement' (Bugg-Levine 2016). This impact investing movement can now be merged with the UN SDG vision for 2030. The creation of SSEs, constitutes an "expensive and long-term market building venture," (OECD 2014, p. 21), but also represents an important aspect of this more general process UN SDG implementation and institutional development.

From the very beginning, a defining feature of impact investing has been what Dadush (2015a, b, p. 173) refers to as 'blueprinting'—the use of templates from conventional finance to create social and sustainable finance. This becomes evident when one juxtaposes some key terminology from both fields: regular investing becomes impact investing, instead of conventional bonds there are social impact bonds, instead of traditional banks—ethical and sustainable banks, instead of credit risk ratings—social impact ratings, return on investment (ROI) becomes social return on investment (SROI), and conventional stock exchanges are re-conceptualized as SSEs. According to Dadush, this systematic imitation has been strategically important to attract a wide range of individuals and institutions by communicating the message that, at the end of the day, impact investing is nothing and now can provide helpful to mainstream impact investing using special SSE exchanges. SSEs are not something altogether alien or out of the ordinary. These attempts to legitimize and popularize impact investing bear a similarity with how investing as such, during the first globalization wave, was conceptualized and promoted as a natural human activity that should be made accessible to everyone (see Preda 2005). Obviously, the current context is very different and the comparison should not be taken literally, but it does help understand the underlying dynamics.

More generally, the emergence and subsequent development of impact investing has been characterized by a deep interest in the quantification and measurability of outcomes to allow for performance-based accountability, while harnessing the 'inherent virtues of the market' to organize and guide the financing of impact-driven entrepreneurship. At the same time, however, there is no universal agreement on whether impact investing, and social finance in general, can be seamlessly integrated with dominant structures and ideology, or whether they might develop into a more fundamental critique of traditional financial and economic ideas (see Lehner 2016a). A full consideration of this issue is beyond the scope of this paper. Suffice it to say that the hybrid character of social finance allows this phenomenon to be conceptualized as a positive redefinition of conventional finance, but also as a potentially problematic application of a particular politico- economic way of thinking in the context of sustainable development and the non-profit economy, making it an extension of some key ideological and economic trends of the past few decades, in particular market-fundamentalism and financialization.

With regard to the structural genesis of social finance, including the opportunities and limitations entailed in SSEs, Glänzel et al. (2013) propose four possible scenarios. First, the Social Investment scenario, or the 'social innovation boom', characterized by large volumes of private investment and the emergence of a broad spectrum of financial instruments and actors. This would eventually include fully developed SSEs, successfully operating in the context of sophisticated regulatory and institutional standards. Second, the Garage Lab scenario in which the supply of finance would exceed the demand, leading to a scattered ecosystem with few scalable projects and the continued importance of more traditional forms of funding. Third, the Commercialization scenario where demand for finance would be relatively high, but it would be met with a restricted supply focused on profitable large scale projects. In such a scenario, the role of SSEs may be commercially significant, although the profit motive would dominate over social and environmental objectives, leaving many high-impact but commercially unattractive initiatives underfunded. And fourth, the Wasteland scenario where, apart from occasional deals and success stories, the field as a whole would remain underdeveloped and marginal, while the majority of social purpose organizations would continue to be dependent on public support and traditional philanthropy.

Figure 2.6 provides an overview of the landscape of impact entrepreneurship and finance, structured around income models and finance instruments most applicable in different sectors of economic activity. Detailed descriptions of the four quadrants can be found in Glänzel et al. (2013, pp. 61–62). Here, it is important to note that the concept of SSEs is not universally applicable across all four quadrants. For example, organizations leaning towards Quadrant 1 and especially Quadrant 2 have limited ability to cover their costs from earned income alone, even though their social or environmental impact may be considerable. In other words, many of these organizations rarely generate positive financial returns, making them dependent on favorable tax laws, private donations, or public subsidies, and thus relatively less attractive to impact investors, most of whom are, at minimum, looking to recover at least their initial investment (GIIN 2016a) (Fig. 3.2).

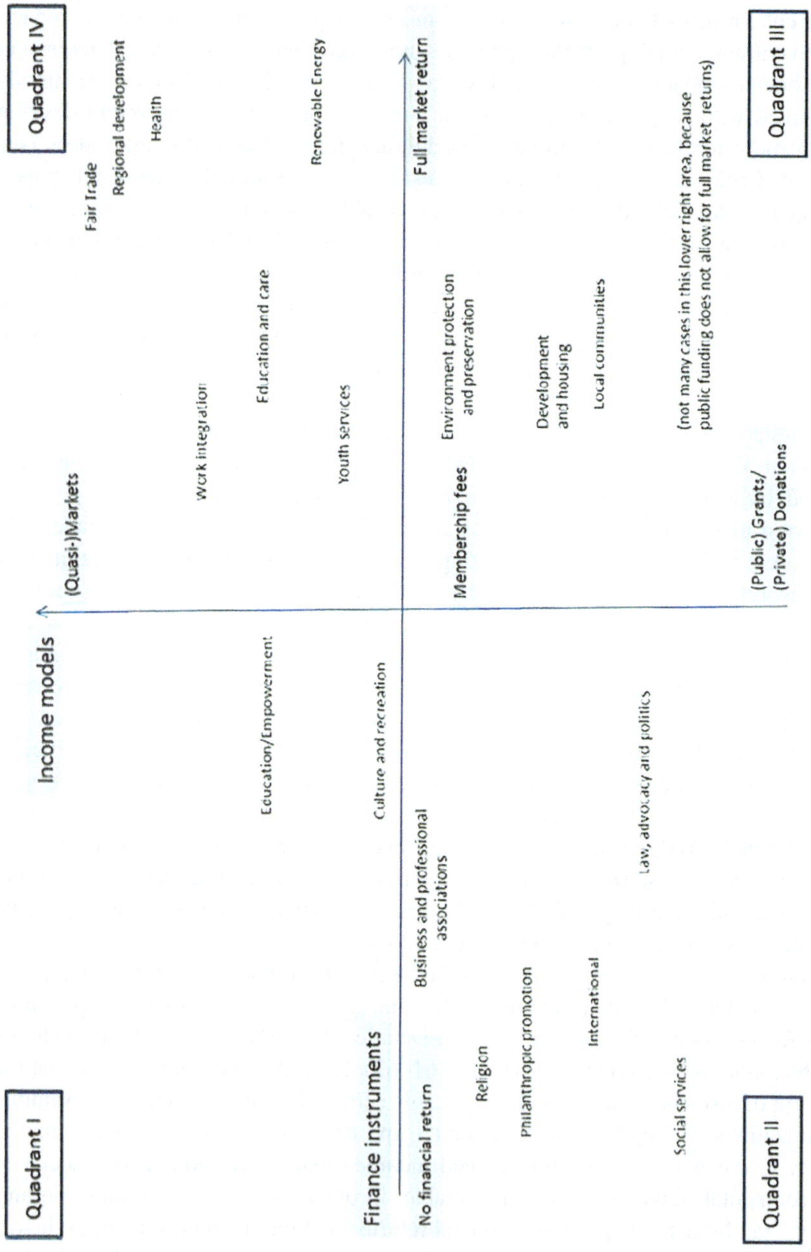

Fig. 3.2 The landscape of social entrepreneurship and finance (Source: Glänzel et al. 2013)

At the moment stock exchanges for social entrepreneurs are missing due to the low deal size. Placing social entrepreneurs in the framework above, the most likely candidates for SSEs can be found in Quadrants III and especially IV. Although services like environmental conservation, education, housing, or energy are often supported by the state, and are not necessarily better organized on a commercial basis, many activities in Quadrants III and IV do involve opportunities for combining positive financial returns with an environmental or social mission. However, as mentioned above, such opportunities do not exist across the whole spectrum covered by Fig. 2.5. For this reason, Glänzel et al. (2013, p. 63) call for a balanced mix of funding mechanisms, and note that although SSEs may prove useful for financing certain types of initiatives, they also have their limits, especially when it comes to activities where success is difficult to define and measure. These caveats are highly relevant in the context of analysing the discourse and activities driving the structural development of impact investing, especially as they relate to the broader economic and political issues mentioned above.

Hartzell (2007, p. 4) asserted in 2007 that "the establishment of an ethical exchange is an idea whose time has come." This conclusion was subsequently echoed by Nicholls & Pharoah (2008, p. 28).

The concept of SSEs has grown out of a gradual confluence of four distinct phenomena. First, there are the ideas and practices of corporate social responsibility (CSR) (Lee 2008; Schmitz & Schrader 2013) and social entrepreneurship (Leadbeater 1997; Poon 2011), both with histories of at least several decades. Second, there are approaches to investment that combine financial objectives with social return: SRI (Sparkes & Cowton 2004; Wallis & Klein 2015), Shared Values—how to reinvent capitalism and unlash a wave of innovation and growth and more recently impact investing (Bugg-Levine and Emerson 2011a, b; WEF 2013; Daggers & Nicholls 2016). Third, there is the reconceptualization of philanthropy over the past couple of decades, characterized by the emergence of 'venture philanthropy' (Letts et al. 1997; Alter et al. 2001; Grossman et al. 2013; Bishop & Green 2015; John & Emerson 2015). And finally, there is the widespread concern for sustainable development (Lélé 1991; Redclift 2005; UN 2015).

Looking into the history there appears to be a clear need for a transparent, clearly regulated market place for impact investing serving the UN SDG goals. This can be derived from what the sector has achieved thus far without the help of market infrastructure assistance. Up to now we see one functioning role model for investors SSEs– the SSX. So what is SSX doing differently from other players? The idea of issuing shares for a social or environmental mission comes from the non-profit sector and still is alive—albeit in a grow linearly mode.

Companies with a social or environmental mission have been issuing shares for several decades. In 1984, the UK-based fair trade company Traidcraft made the first ever public issuance by an ethical business, raising £0.3 million. Over the next couple of decades, many other mission- oriented companies in the UK followed. Of course, none of these businesses offered their shares through a dedicated SSE as no such platform existed. Unless the company was listed on a regular stock exchange, there was also no secondary trading, apart from a few exceptions in which small and relatively inactive 'matched bargain' markets were operated either by the brokerage firm Brewin Dolphin or Triodos Bank. In the early to mid-2000s, in the midst of an increasing number of ethical issuances, Triodos considered opening a single public market, called Ethex, but the idea failed to materialize. Instead, shares of ethical companies kept trading through a matching service provided by Brewin Dolphin (Hartzell 2007, p. 12). Ethex was eventually opened in 2012, and continues to operate as a non-profit online service with secondary trading for some securities, although the platform is not a regulated stock exchange (Ethex 2017). This case provides a useful model for understanding that social stock exchanges are feasible with the will of philanthropy for a limited segment offering limited services and certainly not going as far as being regulated like a traditional stock exchange. A parallel development in the second half of the 1990s was the discussion on the possibility of creating an exchange-type funding platform for non-profit organizations or an index of social enterprises to flag investment opportunities for socially responsible investors (Nicholls & Pharoah 2008, p. 28). According to Emerson & Wachowicz (2000, p. 186), these ideas were first raised in a publication titled "Grants, Debt and Equity: The Non-profit Capital Market and Its Malcontents" (Emerson 1996). By the early 2000s, combined with the popularization of social entrepreneurship and venture philanthropy on the one hand, and the growing discourse on the importance of measurable outcomes and accountability in the non-profit sector on the other, the idea of SSEs as a way to connect mission-oriented organizations with potential investors began gaining some traction. A landmark event took place in 2003 when São Paulo's stock exchange BOVESPA launched the world's first 'social stock exchange'—a project proposed by Celso Grecco and his CSR-focused marketing firm Attitude Social Marketing (Newsweek, 2008).

The idea behind this platform was to use BOVESPA's infrastructure and expertise to connect ethical investors with carefully screened social purpose projects in Brazil that benefitted children and youth in areas of health, literacy, citizenship, education, training, culture, psychosocial care, and environment (Zandee 2004). Importantly, the system involved no transfer of ownership or secondary trading—the return on investment was purely social, making the exchange more of a crowd-donation platform, albeit with specific listing and reporting requirements and as of early 2017, the platform continues to operate as the Socio-Environmental Investment Exchange (BVSA). From BOVESPA's point of view, the project served an important marketing function, as the exchange was looking to improve its public image, explain the operations of a stock exchange to the general public, and thereby attract more people to invest and trade in conventional securities (Zandee 2004).

The BOVESPA SSE, with a stamp of approval from UNESCO and the UN Global Compact, attracted interest not just from other countries in the region but from around the world. In June 2006, a similar project was launched in South Africa—the South African Social Investment Exchange (SASIX) (see CSR 2006; BSA 2006; and Chhichhia 2014, pp. 5–9 for an overview). However, despite the initial plan of developing SASIX into the world's first fully independent SSE (Fury 2010), as of 2017, the platform no longer exists.

Also in the mid-2000s, inspired by these early experiments, a model for a globally standardized social investment market was being developed by a think tank called GEXSI—the Global Exchange for Social Investment. As discussed by Hartigan (2006), this attempt was met with the difficulty of establishing universally accepted performance criteria for listed entities as well as an appropriate accreditation process to generate deal flow. As part of the GEXSI initiative, SSEs were being considered in a number of countries in Europe, Africa, Latin America, and Asia (GEXSI 2017). The idea was to create a global network of platforms focused on funding early-stage projects to help them scale, and thereby make them more attractive to other forms of financing. However, the demand was not sufficient for any of these initiatives to become fully realized (Fury 2010). There might be several reasons why GEXSI did not scale as anticipated. First of all, it was a charity platform and therefore attracted a different kind of "investor". GEXSI grew out of a panel discussion on social entrepreneurship at the WEF in Davos, Switzerland in 2002. Investors who were ready and willing to support worthy charities expressed frustration at the difficulty of evaluating charitable projects. While these investors were not looking for a financial return, they did want to maximize the social benefits generated by their investment. Toward this end, they wanted to analyze charitable organizations as rigorously as they assessed for-profit companies. .platform was only serving the primary market. Therefore GEXSI can be seen more as a complementary stock exchange for not for profit organizations, helping to focus on making charity organizations investment ready as well as help to organize and work on the investment-readiness of not for profit special interest projects like biodiversity conservation but is currently not able to attract capital from traditional investors as in first place charities need to get investment-ready in order to qualify for listing.

Meanwhile in the UK, the topic of SSEs was being actively discussed in reports issued by the Social Investment Taskforce (see Chhichhia 2014, pp. 3–5) and at events such as the 2006 Skoll Forum (Hartzell 2007, p. 12; cf. Wheeler 2006). These discussions were followed by the publication of a report by the New Economics Foundation titled Developing a Social Equity Capital Market which, among other things, discussed the main fundraising obstacles of social enterprises and offered recommendations for developing a more effective market for both primary funding and secondary trading—"essentially a social stock exchange that's fit for the needs of the sector" (NEF 2006, p. 6). The report emphasized the need, possibly in partnership with existing exchanges and intermediaries, to establish a common information point, transparent reporting standards, an accreditation process, a network of supportive roles such as social auditors and advisers, and rules and regulations to minimize the threats of speculation and commercialization.

Whereas both the BOVESPA SSE and SASIX were oriented primarily toward mobilizing funds for non-profit organizations, the discussion in the UK was much more focused on companies that combined for-profit activities with a social or environmental mission. This is clearly evident in the landmark publication by Hartzell (2007), ownership structure (cf. Aggrawal & Dahiya 2006), daily running of SSEs, the complexities of price determination, and the need to develop methods for evaluating the social and environmental performance of the listed firms (cf. Barman 2015) and the subsequent development of impact measurement tools such as IRIS and GIIRS) are the key success factors of such an SSE market place. The London SSX therefore details its mission on its website as follows: "Our mission is to create an efficient, universally accessible buyers' and sellers' public market place where investors and businesses of all sizes can aim to achieve greater impact either through capital allocation or capital raising".

Through a unique partnership with regulated investment exchange NEX, the Social Stock Exchange is the only venue of its kind in the world to give impact businesses of all sizes the opportunity to access public financial markets, thus maximising their capital raising and growth potential. "So the intention is clear: it is a double blind auction system, designed for businesses and investors seeking to create impact through their core business activity, or through investment and it is for profit. It is regulated, so the regulators is responsible when listing the asset, that the criteria of the Social stock Exchange with regard to financials and impact have been met.

In February 2009, a conference initiated by GreaterGood—a South African trust that in 2006 had launched SASIX—met in Bellagio, Italy. The goal was to discuss the possibility of creating a global coordinating body for SSEs—a Global Social Investment Exchange (GSIX), similar in its structure and functions to the World Federation of Exchanges (Alliance 2009). Although no such organization emerged, with support from the Rockefeller Foundation and various family offices, the idea of SSEs continued to be explored in a number of countries (Campanale 2010).

In addition to SSX there are a number of additional smaller initiatives to be mentioned, which are thus far too small to be evaluated in a meaningful manner. This includes the Kenya Social Investment Exchange (KSIX) (see Alliance 2010; Butunyi 2011) and the Portuguese Social Stock Exchange (BVS) (see Costa & Carvalho 2012; Bernardino & Santos 2015; Bernardino et al. 2015).

There have also been reports of planned SSEs in Germany, India, Singapore, New Zealand, Colombia, Thailand, and the US (see Newsweek 2008; Heinecke et al. 2011, p. 56; RGB 2011; Abraham 2013; Socialab 2013; Chhichhia 2014; Shahnaz et al. 2014; Wilson 2014), but none of these seem to have gotten much further from the drawing board.[1]

Another SSE that is regulated and seems to take up speed is NeXii. In 2011, a South African social enterprise advisory firm NeXii, in collaboration with the Stock Exchange of Mauritius (SEM), received regulatory approval to open the world's first stock exchange dedicated entirely to impact investing, called Impact Exchange (IX) (Field 2012; Shahnaz et al. 2014, p. 152). Also in 2011, a private placement platform Impact Partners was launched in Singapore by the Impact Investment Exchange Asia (IIX) to connect social entrepreneurs and impact investors in the

[1] A conceptually related development in the late 2000s was the launch of the Sustainable Stock Exchanges Initiative by the UN (see http://www.sseinitiative.org), a learning platform to encourage the integration of environmental, social and governance (ESG) considerations into the rules and procedures of conventional stock exchanges. A full consideration of this topic is beyond the scope of this paper.

Asia Pacific region. In 2013, NeXii and IIX agreed to collaborate and subsequently merged their efforts to create a fully regulated SSE under SEM—the IX (IIX 2013; Shahnaz et al. 2014, p. 152; OECD 2015, p. 30). In June the same year, the Social Stock Exchange (SSX) opened in London, initially as a platform to aggregate information on publicly listed impact companies but with a clear aspiration to become a fully fledged SSE regulated by the Financial Conduct Authority (FCA) in the future (Shahnaz et al. 2014, p. 152). Later in the year, a private placement platform called the Social Venture Connexion (SVX) opened in Canada, allowing accredited impact investors to connect with local mission- oriented companies (see Spence & Sinopoli 2013; SVX 2013; and Ritchie & Emes 2014 for an overview). Backed by the Ontario government, this initiative was originally proposed as early as 2007 (Floyd 2013) and has subsequently expanded to Mexico (Spence 2014).

3.4 Social Stock Exchanges and Their Challenges

The successful scaling up of SSEs—understood as both primary and secondary trading platforms for securities issued by impact companies—is dependent on a number of enabling conditions and contextual factors. To begin with, there needs to a broad enough consensus among various stakeholders that SSEs are both necessary and effective in addressing the real needs of impact companies and investors. Whether this will translate into successful scaling depends on the degree of ecosystem synergies and patient financial and political support.

A fully operational SSE would need to perform a variety of functions, such as bring new issues to market, support impact companies in finding and securing start-up finance, attract new investors, provide training to companies in regulatory and compliance issues, and generate liquidity, thus offering the opportunity for investors to disinvest. Performing all these functions requires that SSEs themselves are sufficiently funded. As discussed by Hartzell (2007, pp. 24–25), SSEs should ultimately be capable of financing themselves through membership and brokerage fees, as well as various professional and marketing services that they could offer to both businesses and investors. In short, an important condition for the success of SSEs is their financial self-sufficiency and be able to charge market rates for their services (Nicholls & Pharoah 2008, p. 29). Before SSX became operative, Mendell & Barbosa (2013) compares six SSEs that existed in the early 2010s and identifies the key barriers and challenges for their future development, such as the problem of transfers of ownership, lack of appropriate legislative and institutional frameworks, low deal flow and liquidity, and the need to develop a more diverse set of financial products to serve the varying needs of different impact companies. Shahnaz et al. (2014) provide a more general introduction to social and environmental exchanges, including the regulatory status. Environmental exchanges, including the regulatory status and operational mechanics of those that existed in the early 2010s. Dadush (2015a, b) takes a more critical approach, focusing on the regulatory risks and challenges associated with SSEs which she identifies as 'transnational rulemaking laboratories for social finance'. After reviewing the governance of three existing SSEs—IX, SSX, and SVX—Dadush argues that none of these impose adequate requirements when it comes to protecting the interests of not only investors and investees, but also the ultimate beneficiaries of impact investing, i.e. the affected communities.

An important decision in setting up an SSE is whether to establish it as a freestanding structure or as part of an existing stock exchange. This decision may turn out to have implications for avoiding certain threats and challenges later down the road, although both alternatives have their immediate advantages and downsides. Connecting the SSE to an existing exchange has the benefit of allowing access to its infrastructure and technology, thus reducing costs and accelerating the initial setup. So far, this has been the approach taken by most SSEs. However, such a strategy may be discouraging to companies that are worried about risks associated with conventional stock markets. Given that the culture and governance of traditional stock exchanges may not be acceptable to at least some impact companies and their ethically driven investors (Hartzell 2007, p. 7), an SSE that is connected to an existing exchange should operate as a separate board with its own listing and reporting requirements (Shahnaz et al. 2014, pp. 157–159).

Setting appropriate eligibility and reporting criteria, and the governance of SSEs in general, are themselves essential determinants of their success. Theoretically, SSEs could be instrumental in creating a sophisticated, transparent, and widely applicable impact measurement and reporting framework for mission-oriented businesses, perhaps with the assistance and continued monitoring of dedicated rating agencies (Egan 2011). Becoming listed on an SSE would require going through a highly customized due diligence process, while staying listed would be conditional on regular standardized reporting on how well the company is serving its social or environmental mission. These mechanisms are of key importance in determining the attractiveness of SSEs to both impact companies and investors (Campanale 2010). Similarly, rules must be in place to coordinate trading, settlement, clearance, and other key operations.

One of the most decisive factors in determining the long-term success of SSEs is their ability to attract new issuances. This is at least partly a function of the types of securities handled by the exchange—a more diverse set of securities would attract a larger group of companies with different financing needs. Similarly, the less the SSE limits itself to particular areas (e.g. renewable energy, healthcare, housing, etc.) the broader the spectrum of potential issuers, leading to bigger deal flow. At the same time, some impact companies may be discouraged to list on SSEs. For example, they may see engaging with a liquid market place as an encouragement to their investors to disinvest, or it may seem to them too costly, especially if the company is not planning to make additional issues in the future. Founders and management may also fear losing control of their company, or the excessive pressure to become more profitable (Hartzell 2007, p. 26).

It is interesting to note that a widely acknowledged challenge among impact investing practitioners is the alleged lack of investment-ready projects and companies (Bertelsmann Stiftung 2016; FASE 2016; GIIN 2016a). This points to a need for capacity-building assistance for social and green entrepreneurs. For example, SSEs could provide services that encourage the creation of new impact companies and raise the professional capacity of existing ones, thus increasing the number of potential issuers. This would include training and support for meeting the strict listing and reporting requirements, a feature of SSEs that demands considerable commitment and resources from companies. As pointed out by Shahnaz et al. (2014, p. 156), operating a fully regulated SSE entails "striking a balance between the benefits to the investors of access to complete information and the corresponding costs to social enterprises of providing rigorous disclosure."

The flipside of a critical mass of issuers is the demand from investors. As mentioned above, the trend here seems to be positive and thus supportive of the future growth of SSEs. The option of secondary trading is also likely to attract additional investors. Whether the demand for impact assets is sustained over time depends not only on the success of impact companies, but also the motivations and characteristics of impact investors. Here, Gödker & Mertins (2015) offer a useful discussion, pointing out that researchers do not yet have a good enough understanding of what drives impact decisions, although it seems to be a mix of personal values, identity, and political orientation on the one hand, and expectations regarding return, principles of diversification, and the use of internalized heuristics about investing on the other. A noteworthy recent development with regard to investor behavior is the emergence of '100% impact' investors who have committed their whole portfolio to impact assets (Toniic 2016). A growing number of such investors could certainly have a considerable effect on the future development of SSEs.

A defining feature of most organizations in the fields of social entrepreneurship and finance is hybridity—trying to combine the goals, principles and methods of business with those traditionally associated with the non-profit sector (Birkholz 2015). In many ways, SSEs represent a perfect case study of what this might entail in practice. The growth of SSEs is therefore also dependent on how well these institutions combine ideas and practices that may sometimes be difficult to reconcile (see Hartigan 2006). If SSEs fail in maintaining the delicate balance between the rationales of 'profit' and 'impact', they may risk alienating certain investors and companies whose active participation may be essential for the long-term success of SSEs. In other words, 'success' may mean different things for different stakeholders. Therefore a universal underlying framework as provided by the UN SDGs is helpful in defining success in a manner that is not arbitrary. As emphasized by Dadush (2015a, b), merely quantitative measures (e.g. deal flow), although important, may not be sufficient to assess the overall performance of SSEs, as many investors and investees may give equal weight to mission alignment, ethical integrity, and whether the SSE itself is ran as a social enterprise which all are expressions of their ToC. Here, healthy competition between SSEs would help ensure that both investors and businesses have the option to choose a platform that is best aligned with their values and purposes.

And finally, effective regulation is another key determinant of the long-term success of SSEs and social finance in general (see Addis 2015). On the one hand, SSEs are embedded in existing judicial frameworks and must therefore abide by the rules and regulations that apply to the legal form that a particular SSE has taken. On the other hand, they are innovative platforms that have considerable self-regulatory leeway. In many ways, SSEs currently under development will set the regulatory standard for years to come. And since these platforms bring together a variety of actors and organizations, this may have far-reaching implications not just for SSEs, but for the social enterprise and impact investing sectors more broadly. As pointed out by Dadush (2015a, b), merely 'blueprinting' the regulatory model of conventional stock exchanges may prove to be highly problematic and potentially even undermine the fundamental purpose of SSEs.

A more critical interpretation would see the emergence of SSEs as the result of applying a particular politico-economic way of thinking in areas that have traditionally been associated with philanthropic giving and the activities of non-profit organizations, often within the context of considerable state presence; and as a symptom of financialization—the growing role of financial motives, actors, markets, and institutions in the operations of the economy and society at large (Epstein 2005, p. 4; see also Thümler 2016; Dowling 2017). According to this interpretation, social purpose organizations are increasingly subjugated to the financial logic of the market while 'positive impact' is turned into a commodified investment opportunity; from a financing point of view, marketable solutions become preferred over alternatives for which it is difficult to present a profitable business case (Dadush 2015a, b, pp. 152–154; cf. The Economist 2006). For many philantropists however this may be a desired development, as it allows them to use a philantopic coin many times. At the moment the grant scheme is set up in a way, that a coin can be only spent once. When spent it is gone and it is not recuperated to be used again. So the grant scheme does not allow for an informed financial decision where to best spent the philanthropic coin. This is where it can be recouped after a certain time which make projects more transparent and accountable for their success and prevents the waste of grant money. The grant and not for profit scheme has been described as a dictator game in behavioural economics.

Another argument is the shift from traditional philanthropy to philanthro-capitalism (Bishop & Green 2015) may be ultimately followed by a shift from philanthro-capitalism to 'quarterly philanthro- capitalism' where entrepreneurial activity and managerial decision-making become increasingly affected by the dictates of investors and social finance institutions, including SSEs. This shift is driven by the often unshakable belief that the 'forces of the market' (including the financial market) can be successfully harnessed to tackle almost any social or environmental problem. Although this is certainly true in a number of areas, market fundamentalism combined with the mentality and methods borrowed from the world of finance may also lead to some negative consequences (see Jacobs & Mazzucato 2016)—in this sense, the 'impact economy' (Martin 2016) is no different from the rest of the economy. These potentially negative consequences represent legitimate threats to SSEs and avoiding them is a key challenge in the future development of these platforms, as well as social entrepreneurship and impact investing in general.

For example, just like traditional venture capital is often tempted to make speculative gains through a quick exit on a stock exchange (Lazonick & Mazzucato

2012, pp. 13–15), assuming that the demand for impact assets continues to grow (see GIIN 2016b for an overview of recent market trends), venture philanthropists and other early-stage investors may become increasingly inclined to float impact companies on SSEs in ways that primarily benefit insiders. Strict regulation will be required together with regulating market access to create the respective governance and prevent insider trading. And similar to conventional stock exchanges, regular reporting of both financial and impact data within the context of highly liquid secondary markets will inevitably create short-term pressures to meet the expectations of investors, analysts, and rating agencies, possibly at the expense of long-term goals and planning. As discussed above, such a system has a number of important strengths and benefits. However it likewise can create pressures to commercialize, rivalry between ownership and control, mission drift, and a variety of conflicts of interest, including those involved in underwriting and market making (see Ellis et al. 2000; Aggrawal 2002).

The degree to which these threats translate into actual practice depends on, first, whether there will be a 'social innovation boom' (Glänzel et al. 2013), leading to a critical mass of profitable impact companies, and second, the evolution of the rules and regulations that are going to govern the operations of SSEs, and by extension, the activities of listed companies and their investors. As emphasized by Hartzell (2007, p. 4), SSEs must be "carefully crafted so that [they are] protected against the exploitation for private benefit, but still remain flexible enough to be treated as genuine exchanges by investors." In other words, the hybrid nature of SSEs requires the development of innovative regulatory frameworks and principles of governance, the purpose of which would be to ensure that the investment and trading activity on SSEs does not become decoupled from the underlying purpose of the listed firms and that the rights and interests of other stakeholders are well-represented alongside those of investors and investees.

Dadush (2015a, b) has offered a number of recommendations, such as careful design of listing and reporting requirements, explicitly identifying what constitutes malpractice, establishing procedures for the effective enforcement of rules of conduct, setting up safeguards to limit short-termist investor behavior and mission-diluting commercialization, and perhaps most importantly, adopting a definition of success for SSEs that includes the protection of beneficiary interests. SSEs are yet to prove their long-term viability and potential for funding impact companies in volumes that would have a noticeable effect on the real economy. However, the future trajectory of SSEs will be determined by decisions made during setup, some of which may become increasingly difficult to revise later down the road.

As of April 2019, there are six SSEs under active development: BVSA, BRiiX, SVX, IX, GIIVX, and SSX. The first is the continuation of the initial BOVESPA project, making it essentially a donation platform. The second began as a consulting company, and now acts as an information portal for connecting impact investors with companies showcased on BRiiX, of which there are currently five. SVX is registered with the Ontario Securities Commission as a restricted dealer, making it a private placement platform that connects accredited investors with local impact ventures. A new SVX platform was scheduled to open in early 2017, but this has been postponed to later in the year. Meanwhile, an affiliate of SVX was launched in Mexico in 2015, which is currently focused on offering educational services on impact investing. In terms of building a publicly accessible market place for securities issued by social or green enterprises, both BRiiX and SVX are still in the early stages of their development.

The Singapore-based organization IIX re-branded themselves in early 2017 and announced plans to expand globally (IIX 2017). The activities of IIX are built around four institutional structures. First, there is the IIX Impact Accelerator, targeting early-stage social enterprises in South and Southeast Asia, helping them with seed finance and capacity building. Second, IIX operates a private placement platform called Impact Partners that connects accredited investors with impact companies. Third, IIX manages an equity investment fund called IIX Growth Fund. And finally, there is the public trading platform IX, operating as a separate board of SEM. As of April 2017, there is very little activity on the IX, with only one product listed, the Women's Livelihood Bond, and the exchange does not seem to be a current priority of IIX (cf. Dadush 2015a, b, pp. 209–210).

The Vienna-based Global Impact Investing Foundation (GIIF), in collaboration with the United Nations Industrial Development Organization (UNIDO), is planning to launch a global impact investing platform GIIVX later in 2017. The investment themes on GIIVX are organized around the UN Sustainable Development Goals (SDGs), providing the platform with a wide but easy to understand categorization for the listed initiatives. Impact entrepreneurs will be able to showcase verified projects on the GIIVX website, while agreements are negotiated between investors and investees using the contract documentation and support tools provided by GIIVX. According to its website, GIIVX is also working on developing a new standardized tool for impact measurement that can be used by investors to evaluate the projects listed on GIIVX.

To date, the most highly developed and active SSE is the London-based SSX. The platform is open to impact companies from anywhere in the world, as long as they meet SSX's listing requirements. As of April 2017, SSX is registered as a UK Limited Company, making it a for-profit enterprise. In addition, SSX is a Recognized Investment Exchange, regulated by the UK Financial Conduct Authority (FCA). This was achieved through a partnership with NEX Exchange (formerly ISDX) which made it a segment of NEX where the securities of SSX-listed companies are now being traded. Alternatively, listed companies can have their shares traded either on the London AIM market or the London Stock Exchange (LSE) main market (All Street Research 2017, p. 15). Although the SSX lists about 50 companies, only 12 of those can be traded. The remaining are private businesses who are currently showcasing their activities through SSX, although they may issue tradable securities in the future. The SSX is also planning to open small localized exchanges, similar to that of their South West Social Stock Exchange, to enable more investment in impact companies that are operating at the community level. Pilot projects for such local exchanges have recently been launched in Wirral and Liverpool, with discussions underway in Edinburgh, Scotland (All Street Research 2017, p. 14).

Chapter 4
Critical analysis and Prognosis on the Development of SSEs

4.1 Prognosis on the Development of SSEs

Given that several of the early SSE-type funding platforms have come and gone and most of the remaining ones are limited in size and activity, very little empirical research has been done specifically on SSEs. However, the recent growth of SSX in the UK, continued work on BVSA, IX, BRiiX, and SVX in Mexico, as well as the upcoming launch of the new SVX in Canada and GIIVX in Austria, may in the near- and mid-term future provide increasing opportunities for studying the nature and operations of these platforms and their relationship to the broader field of impact entrepreneurship and investing. At the same time the UN SDG may function as a game changer as they establish a vision, a ToC and a universally agreed impact goal endorsed by 194 member states, which helps in creating a level playing field in the financial sector at least for the impact investing segment.

Concerning the characteristics of SSEs compared to conventional stock exchanges, the only SSE active enough to allow for at least some meaningful comparison is the SSX in the UK. From a practitioner's point of view, SSX will certainly help inform the design of similar platforms elsewhere.

The study of impact investor behavior creates a bridge between the sociology and economics of SSEs. For example, what characterizes the investors who are attracted to SSE-type investment platforms (e.g. Millennials) and what prevents institutional investors (e.g. funds) from accessing impact investing? The analysis thus far shows that besides the SSX there has been little attempt to set up an SSE which is for profit. When continued successfully as the current volumes seem to suggest it can serve as a blueprint for other "for profit SSEs". ISSX solves the problem of retail investors that now for the first time have the chance to invest in impact, if they wish. An open issue is how pension funds can be attracted as they need higher lot sizes due to regulation and policy. Another open issue needing research is what are the corresponding implications for portfolio theory, social and sustainable investing in general, and the future development of the impact economy? In a similar vein, it would be

K. Wendt, *Social Stock Exchanges*, Sustainable Finance,
https://doi.org/10.1007/978-3-030-99720-5_4

interesting to know the profile of the ventures listed on SSEs and which of them are most successful, both financially and in terms of their social and environmental performance. A connected and potentially important sub-theme is the relationship between impact investing and innovation. In the future, SSEs could theoretically play a supportive role in mobilizing finance for growth companies in areas such as renewable energy, sustainable engineering, electric mobility, green materials, and biotechnology all in line with the UN SDGs, which underscore the SSE market. Impact investing and SSEs could also play a considerable role in directing development finance and find models to enhance development aid through public private partnership schemes. It appears that this is the goal of GIIVX in Vienna who has UNIDO as a strategic partner. If SSEs indeed become a channel for cross-border investment for sustainable development, this in itself would open up a whole new area of GDP growth and empirical research.

Building on the early papers by Dadush (2015a, b) and Burand (2015), more work could be done on the regulatory, legal and policy implications of impact investing and SSEs, including the assessment of existing regulatory gaps and potential policy incentives. There is also ample room for SSE-related theoretical research, especially when examined in the broader context of social and sustainable finance (see Lehner 2016b). For example, do SSEs represent a more fundamental shift in the relationship between business, investment and society – a prelude for a future in which most companies and investors combine the profit-motive with social and environmental objectives?

This being said however, it appears that SSEs will complement existing stock and bond exchanges for smaller size assets, as a seedbed for the market, where survivors can then leave the black box of venture capital and private equity when they have grown strong enough. However while SSEx are increasing the offer side by listing investees and make them more salient, the figures and quantifications behind these assets remain an issue of concern. Only few assets really have establishe Key Prerformance Indicatores, defined impact, include a thorough and across SSES comparable impact assessment and reporting scheme, most of them fail to quantify and measure impact which makes it impossible for institutional invetors to invest tinto them (besides the problems of lot size and fungability). Therefore a clear scheme and framework on which all existing SSEs agree to increase fungability, a shared system to be able to measure survivor bias, a clear and shared set of KPIs for impact (less is more, so choose 3 or 3 and then collect the data and create the data analysis), clear listing criteria that require minimum standards for impact assessments, reporting, KPIs and big data collection on the real impact on the ground would help the market a step further in tow waqys:

4.2 Recommendations for an Ecosystems Approach of SSEs

Step one: First of all when SSEs collaborate and harmonize their listing criteria, assement and reporting standards as well as the impact KPIs ther asset class becomes more fungible. If this has been achieved special impact funds can be created not on a black box, but a transparent lsting approach and their performance and survivor bias can be compared to other SRI funds.

Step two: It is still a much further step to go to enable traditional stock exchanges to develop impact investments in their primary market function to a point where the impact assets can be listed – perhaps at a special segment on the traditional stock exchanges which again would increase transparency, intercomparability, salience, key performance indicators data collection and quantification of impact and therefore boost the market, calculate the survivor bias, make the impact investment market more scalable as new investor classes like institutional investors now can be invited and have a chance to invest in a market that it fungible, has depth and breath and enjoys real market making. They also will profit from the metrics like tracking error of impact funds (which can be created as a result of Step one) against SRIs and EU Article) funds (funds that are aligned with the green taxonomy.

The green and social taxonomies of the Eu currently are short of assets that fulfil their requirements. If the market gets more aligned and the SSEs become under a unified framework the breathing ground of eco-social impact assets and the market has a seamless approach to growing this breathing ground from seed to venture to private equity under a unified framework and clear shared criteria topped up with measurements on survivor bias, impact promised and achieved so the construction of meaningful impact funds becomes possible and measurable against market criteria including the publication of a Tracking Error against an Article 8 (SRI) or Article 9 Fund in accordance with the EU Sustainable Finance Disclorure Regulation) the market can develop in a transparent and salient way from small size alternative asset listed on an SSE combined through – transparency, salience and quantifications—to the fund industry which is bound by fiduciary duties and therefore very strict when it comes to quantification and comparison. When Social Stock Exchanges are aligning and open to contribute to the ecosystem of liquid markets by providing the salience, metrics, transparency, traceability, harmonized impact investings, impact reportings and impact measurement, calculations of survivors bias and tracking errors against SRI and Article 9 funds a market development gap can be closed due to the ecosystem element that SSEs then will constitute and help the market and impact assets to evolve. This also means leaving an idiosyncratic perspective and move to an allocentric market perspective which definitely will entail a (mind) systems change.

The question how to create a functioning impact market with enough investment ready deals, state of the art due diligence and enough capital to absorb it remains a top priority, if one wants impact investing to deliver on its promise to be the key for resolving global challenges in a time where the traditional levers of change, including philanthropy and government aid, are insufficient to address the critical issues of our time. Therefore the market mechanisms to translate a compelling concept into a sound market strategy populating both the filed of impact investors in search for assets as well sustainable entrepreneurs in search for capital while making sure the assets are investment-ready in a traditional investment based approach, the rules of the games are clear and met, traditional due diligence is done and potentially complemented by additional layers and a liquid market place is available.

According to Brandstetter & Lehner (2015) investors struggle to allocate capital towards the social sector, because the above proposed performance measurement metrics do neither fully assess risks associated with the generation of impact nor consider relationships and interdependencies between parameters of risks and return. This becomes an aggravated problem when looking at a portfolio level, due to inevitable co-variances that remain unaccounted for (Brandstetter & Lehner 2015). Portfolio models can only be applied in situations where risk and return metrics are accurately measurable and comparable. According to the academic research undertaken so far, some researchers find that "Unfortunately, such consistent metrics are largely absent within the emergent field of social finance" (Geobey, Westley, and Weber 2012). According to Brandstetter & Lehner (2015) "Therefore, since an optimized asset allocation is an indispensable necessity for institutional investors, the expected market growth of impact investing will be dampened as long as impact investments' characteristics do not match conventional portfolio tools." One question therefore is how can impact investment characteristics meet conventional portfolio tools, or alternatively the regulatory board of a stock exchange sets the rules for impact measurement based on a universally shared framework. Scientific researchers acknowledge that "Across sectors, there are already a number of measurement systems in use, endorsed by various impact investing actors. Among them are the Impact Reporting and Investment Standards (IRIS), the Global Impact Investing Rating System (GIIRS) and the B Impact Assessment powered by B Lab "(Antadze and Westley 2012; Jackson 2013). Those standards can be used to inform the regulation on impact definition and management even more so as for now the UN SDGs can provide the underlying universal framework.

An open question is whether a double auction process could help to resolve the problem of investment ready assets and the investment gap while impact investors are sitting on piles of money to be invested in the market. The Nasdaq defines a double auction Systems by which listed securities are bought and sold through brokers on the securities exchanges, as distinguished from the OTC market, where trades are negotiated. Unlike the conventional auction with one auctioneer and many buyers, double auction markets consist of many sellers and many buyers.

Again, this requires the creation of "listed securities".

Could the implementation of the UN SDG justify an own market place? Would such a market place help address the investment gap in impact investing?

Could the application of universal measurement criteria based on SDGs create a level playing field in measuring impact? Such a level playing field could be a necessary and required preliminary to a double auction system. At the moment there is a wealth of impact measurement tools, techniques and criteria. For creation of a market place a universally agreed ToC as provided by the SDGs could provide helpful in creating a transparent double auction market place. SSEs then could be regulated on the basis of such a universally shared model. Creating such a level playing field may be a feasible way forward.

While philanthropy has been playing an important role in setting up impact investing, the global challenge is beyond the means of this investor. Framed in this way impact investing has to become not only compatible with traditional investment, but be provided with the same set of structural support in order to make it grow.

How could Impact investing therefore draw from the advantages of double bind auction systems and could Nasdaq be seen as a role model for SSEs in setting the right framework and putting the right systems in place for enabling and growing social innovation, the way Nasdaq was promoting technical innovation. The question may be beyond this paper, but as a start it is useful to look into the advantages of double blind auction systems and analyse what can be learned from the so far existing SSEs.

4.3 Outlook

At the moment only financial capital is valuated at stock exchanges. The other dimensions which forms basis of the green, brown and social taxonomy of the EU or the viable systems framework are not explicitely valued in a coherent manner, the pricing mechanismmay not be entirely efficient in particular when it comes to alternative assets (venture capital, seed an private equity). The prices here may be distorted and at least are a black box, leaving questions like survivor bias, valuation, fair and transparent value, fungability and impact definition, management measurement and quantification open.. The analysis took two directions: At first, to gain understanding to what extent practitioners and researcher might find usefulness in In another step the autor was looking into whether inclusion of an ISE/SSE in an ecosystem approach can make the and finaly through the ecosystem approach make the financial ecosystem more hole, close a gap, make impact investing more investible and attractive for mainstream investors Trought a clear ecssystem approach that makes unknown variables transparent like survivor bias, like tracking error, like impact listing criteria and impact quantification helps eco-social impact assets to grow beyond the alternative asset status in a salient and transparent manner and finally help the primary market function of traditional stock exchanges to pick up assets when they reached a certain size. Secondly traditional stock exchanges when they participate in the ecosystem approach can help impact assets through the listing process at a traditional stock exchange through the process of education and participation in ecosystem creation finally leading to a listing on a regulates stock exchange or a special impact segment at a traditional stock exchange. This requires not only the harmonization of SSEs and their listing criteria, impact assessments and valuations, but also the extension of the field to a multi-acteurs network including the traditional stock exchanges, venture fund and traditional asset managers. An ecosystems build in a way that shows the asset development process from seed to SSE listing to primary market function could have a signalling function for investors and investees and hold the promise of a fair and transparent valuation. Another direction could address the question under what conditions institutional investors can access impact investing market at transaction costs comparable to share price analysis and due diligence service costs (currently they would have to engage in costs for searching and finders fees) or whether and in what ways an ISE/SSE listing segment with clear criteria supported by a market making function to guarantee liquidity could enhance invest-ability of impact investments for institutional investor. Pension funds are now required to include impact investing in their mandates (e.g. Norwegian Pension Fund), but do not have the possibility to invest in the market as currently shaped, due to lot size of impact deals and other fiduciary issues (Wendt 2020). Pension capital under fiduciary management has been 51 trillion USD in 2020 according to OECD (OECD 2020), so solving this investment deadlock for institutional investors appears to be one of the most appealing questions in the current impact market. This finding leads the author to focus on the institutional side and therefore the four research questions formulated above.

Chapter 5
Conclusions and Limitations

This work offered analyzed the impact investing landscape by using a double perspective both theoretical and practical. The interviews provide interesting insights for future studies. Although impact investing is still in the early stages of its development, the growing interest from mainstream financial institutions signal that the field is no longer merely an interesting idea in the minds of a few devoted enthusiasts.

The literature review confirms that there are several instruments and approaches that can be used to make a positive impact in the society. A close connections between social enterprises and impact investing has been detected. With regard to allocation of assets on the secondary market, regulated exchanges little has been known why investors shy away from placing their assets to the market in form of an ICO or IPO. In this regard the interviews offered useful insight in identifying small lot sizes, start up or early growth stage of the assets and fiduciary duties as hindrances to listing assets. Also no commonly agreed set of listing criteria exists.. For this reason, the interviews offer several important insights for future studies.

With regard to the future study of SSEs, when placed within the general context of social and sustainable finance, there is already considerable room for SSE-related theoretical, legal and policy research. Options for empirical research are currently limited, simply because most SSEs are still relatively small. However, there does exist a critical mass of impact investors, while impact assets still have to be further developed and nourished by social entrepreneurs, microfinance and growth stage assets.

Although the current study has extended our understanding on impact investments, social stock exchanges and the investment gap, it also has a number of limitations. As with all reviews it was limited by the search terms used and the exclusion criteria. Several working papers and conference proceeding have been excluded from our review due to the fact that they do not represents "scientific knowledge" assessed through peer review. However the publication discussed in this literature review provide a snapshot of research on impact investing, social stock exchanges and social entrepreneurship which is representative of the state of the art

K. Wendt, *Social Stock Exchanges*, Sustainable Finance,
https://doi.org/10.1007/978-3-030-99720-5_5

at the time. From a policy/practitioners perspective, three main conclusions may be drawn from this work:

1. Social stock exchanges for impact investing have a great potential for the growth of social enterprises by offering a wide range of financial instruments that span from equity to debit when they agree on a common framework and define on how they can strengthen the overall financial markets and systems in an ecosystem approach;
2. Social stock exchanges represent a useful instrument to private investors as well investees as they increase the salience of many kind of impact assets;
3. Investors look with great interest at this market. Money is there and waiting to be deployed to impact assets as soon as the inconsistencies and inefficiencies in definition of impact, measurement of impact, reporting of impact and quantification of impact have been reseolved
4. SSEs are currently in their early stages of seedor growth and will need some time to achieve the status of "investable in the secondary market,
5. Due to market incompatibilities institutional investors and investors with fiduciary duties can only invest in green bonds and project bonds following a blended value approach rather than a real impact approach.
6. In order to help classify impact it might be useful to tie and align sustainable finance with the seven capitals model form Flora and Flora.

   For the purpose of SSEs we can cluster Floras 7 capitals framework into KPIs for

(1) Social capital created: defined as Social, cultural relational value, (2) Human competencies development defined as human capital circumscribing the impact on the users, (3) Intellectual Capital gains through education of citizens, stakeholders, patents received, (4) the growth of political capital and political democratic competencies, (5) the growth of environmental capital by avoided CO_2 emissions, climate mitigation, provision and maintaining of ecosystems services. (6) the growth of natural capital the embeddedness in natural environment and therefore the competencies to deal with adaptation (subject to nature) and enhancement of the environment (active improvement approach), (7) the increase in economic capital and financial capital, as well as (8) the increase in physical/manufactured capital like the building and infrastructure benefits and (9) build capital: the ties build through the engagement with the affected communities by the project or asset.

7. Recent views on sustainability by financial organisation use the capitals framework to circumscribe the SDGs. The dynamics can be researched using the viable systems approach if we cluster the capitals into economic, social and environmental The benefit of clustering is that we can keep the triple bottom line logic intact, but at the same time understand the overlaps and dynamics between these three dimensions. This is considered helpful when understanding the impacts and dynamics in implementing SSEs to redirect capital to sustainable growth. Moreover these dimensions are in alignment with the EU definition and Action Plan, as

the EU differentiates between a green, brown and social taxonomy, which can be achieved through sustainable economic growth.

8. There is a synergistic flow of energy among the viable systems dimensions which can be either positive or negative—resulting in the growth or diminishment of capital. When the dimensions foster one another they can fuel a sustainable, self-supporting system that fosters a healthy ecosystem, a vital economy, and social well- being (Flora and Flora 2013). Callaghan and Colton proposed that a society cannot flourish if one of the seven capital is excessively built up at the expense of another, and claimed that a "resilient" society is one that finds the right balance of capitals. We deem that transferable to the clustered model we use here the viable systems approach.
9. Finally, the results of this work have implications for the development of the impact investing market and its instruments. This is true when we consider the market from the offer side and from the demand side. Only with a better understanding of the entire impact investing landscape, the functioning of secondary markets and the related investment opportunities is it possible to ensure an effective market development.

At the moment only financial capital is valuated at stock exchanges. The other dimensions which forms basis of the green, brown and social taxonomy of the EU or the viable systems framework are not explicitely valued in a coherent manner, the pricing mechanism may not be entirely efficient. The analysis could take two directions: At first, to gain understanding to what extent impact investors, foundations, banks and private equity and venture capital investors consider the inclusion of a new ISX/SSX segment at the stock exchanges useful. Or looking into whether inclusion of an ISE/SSE segment can make the market investible and attractive for mainstream investors and investors with fiduciary duties like pension funds and other Institutional Investors., as a listing on a regulates stock exchange could have a signalling function for investors. Another direction could address the question under what conditions institutional investors can access impact investing market at transaction costs comparable to share price analysis and due diligence service costs (currently they would have to engage in costs for searching and finders fees) or whether and in what ways an ISE/SSE listing segment with clear criteria supported by a market making function to guarantee liquidity could enhance invest-ability of impact investments for institutional investor. Pension funds are now required to include impact investing in their mandates (e.g. Norwegian Pension Fund), but do not have the possibility to invest in the market as currently shaped, due to lot size of impact deals and other fiduciary issues (Wendt 2020). Pension capital under fiduciary management has been 51 trillion USD in 2020 according to OECD (OECD 2020), so solving this investment deadlock for institutional investors appears to be one of the most appealing questions in the current impact market. This finding leads the author to focus on the institutional side and therefore the four research questions formulated above.

Finally, the results of this work have implications for the development of the impact investing market and its instruments. This is true when we consider the market from the offer side and from the demand side. Only with a better understanding of the entire impact investing landscape, the functioning of secondary markets and the related investment opportunities is it possible to ensure an effective market development.

References

References Sustainability

Antadze, N., & Westley, F. R. (2012). Impact metrics for social innovation: Barriers or bridges to radical change? *Journal of Social Entrepreneurship, 3*(2), 133–150.

Brest, P., & Born, K. (2013). When can impact investing create real impact. *Stanford Social Innovation Review, 11*(4), 22–31. https://community-wealth.org/sites/clone.community-wealth.org/files/downloads/article-brest-born.pdf

Calandra, D., & Favareto, M. (2020). *Social stock exchange between academics and practitioners' view.* https://www.researchgate.net/publication/343126029_Social_Stock_Exchange_between_academics_and_practitioners%27_view

Carlowitz, H. C. (1680). *Sylvicultura oeconomica.* Orell Füssli. https://www.orellfuessli.ch/shop/home/artikeldetails/A1062461713?ProvID=10917751&gclid=CjwKCAjw7cGUBhA9EiwArBAvohcEuIHscOLn3i4FJWgQF_uY9AZJCucY5VZuEb_JVXhOiT3Faba2UxoCfSgQAvD_BwE

Dinnen, P., & Beach, A. (2018). Compelling reasons and growing evidence of positive impacts from private capital investing in emerging markets. In *Positive impact investing* (pp. 145–162). Springer. https://link.springer.com/chapter/10.1007/978-3-319-10118-7_7

EVPA. (2018). *Impact strategies journey.* Available at https://evpa.eu.com/pages/evpa-impact-strategies-journey

Geobey, S., Westley, F. R., & Weber, O. (2012). Enabling social innovation through developmental social finance. *Journal of Social Entrepreneurship, 3*(2), 151–165.

Geobey, S., & Weber, O. (2013). Lessons in operationalizing social finance: The case of Vancouver City Savings Credit Union. *Journal of Sustainable Finance & Investment, 3*(2), 124–137.

Glänzel, G., & Scheuerle, T. (2016). Social impact investing in Germany: Current impediments from investors' and social entrepreneurs' perspectives. *VOLUNTAS: International Journal of Voluntary and Nonprofit Organizations, 27*(4), 1638–1668.

Glaser, B. G., & Strauss, A. L. (1979). In Hopf & Weingarten (Eds.), *The discovery of object-oriented theory: A basic strategy of qualitative social research.* Qualitative Social Research.

Hebb, T. (2013). Impact investing and responsible investing: What does it mean? *Journal of Sustainable Finance & Investment, 3*(2), 71–74.

Hummels, H., & de Leede, M. (2014). The emergence of impact investments: The case of microfinance. In *Socially responsible investment in the 21st century: Does it make a difference for society?* (pp. 91–115). Emerald Group Publishing Limited.

K. Wendt, *Social Stock Exchanges*, Sustainable Finance,
https://doi.org/10.1007/978-3-030-99720-5

Hummels, H., & Millone, M. (2014). *The social function of asset classes in microfinance* (pp. 162–186). Microfinance Institutions, Palgrave, MacMillan UK.
Jaeggi, O., Webber Ziero, G., Tobin-de la Puente, J., & Kölbel, J. F. (2018). Understanding sustainable finance. In *Positive impact investing* (pp. 39–63). Springer. https://link.springer.com/chapter/10.1007/978-3-319-10118-7_3
Kleissner, C. (2018/2019). Introduction. In K. Wendt (Ed.), *Positive impact investing*. Springer.
Pretorius, L., & Giamporcaro, S. (2012). Sustainable and responsible investment (SRI) in South Africa: A limited adoption of environmental criteria. *Investment Analysts Journal, 75*, 1–19.
Schober, C., & Rauscher, O. (2014). Alle Macht der Wirkungsmessung? In *Forschung zu Zivilgesellschaft, NPOs und Engagement* (pp. 261–281). Springer. https://link.springer.com/chapter/10.1007/978-3-658-06177-7_15
Shulman, J. M., & George, B. (2012). Growing jobs and getting returns: Impact investing through entrepreneurs. *Journal of Global Business Management, 8*(1), 123–132.
SRS. (2018). *Communication on progress*. https://www.unglobalcompact.org/participation/report/cop/create-and-submit/active/425015
Strauss, A. L., & Corbin, J. (1990). *Basics of qualitative research: Grounded theory procedures and techniques*. SAGE.
Suetin, A. (2011). Post-crisis developments in international financial markets. *International Journal of Law and Management, 53*(1), 51–61.
The World Economic Forum WEF. (2013). *Bringing impact investing from the margins to the mainstream*. Available at https://thegiin.org/knowledge/publication/bringing-impact-investing-from-the-margins-to-the-mainstream
Viviers, S., & Firer, C. (2013). Responsible investing in South Africa-a retail perspective. *Journal of Economic and Financial Sciences, 6*(1), 217–242.
Viviers, S., Ratcliffe, T., & Hand, D. (2011). From philanthropy to impact investing: Shifting mindsets in South Africa. *Corporate Ownership and Control, 8*, 25–43. University Press.
Weiss, C. (1995). Nothing as practical as good theory: Exploring theory-based evaluation for comprehensive community initiatives for children and families. In *New approaches to evaluating community initiatives*. Aspen Institute.
Wendt, K. (2020). Social stock exchanges: Defining the research agenda. In *Contemporary issues in sustainable finance* (pp. 79–129). Springer. https://ideas.repec.org/h/pal/psifcp/978-3-030-40248-8_5.html

Internet Sources

Barile. (2018). Sustainability and the viable systems approach: Opportunities and issues for the governance of the territory. *Sustainability, 10*(3), 790.
Barile, S., et al. (2018). Sustainability and the viable systems approach: Opportunities and issues for the governance of the territory. *Sustainability, MDPI, Open Access Journal, 10*(3), 1–17.
European Union. (2019). EU action plan for sustainable growth. Retrieved from https://ec.europa.eu/info/business-economy-euro/banking-and-finance/sustainable-finance_en
Elkington, J. (1997). Partnerships from cannibals with forks. In J. Elkington (Ed.), *Cannibals with forks: The triple bottom line of 21st century business*. Capstone/John Wiley, Hardcover.
Elkington J. (2021): Partnerships from cannibals with forks. Retrieved from https://edisciplinas.usp.br/pluginfile.php/5578099/mod_resource/content/1/Elkington_Triple_Bottom_Line.pdf
Flora, C., & Flora, J. (2013). *Rural communities: Legacy and change* (4th ed.). Westview.
Flora, C. B., Emery, M., Fey, S., & Bregendahl, C. (2005). *Community capitals: A tool for evaluating strategic interventions and projects*. North Central Regional Center for Rural Development. http://wp.aae.wisc.edu/ced/wpcontent/uploads/sites/3/2014/01/204.2-Handout-Community-Capitals.pdf

OECD. (2020). Global pension statistics. Retrieved from https://www.oecd.org/finance/globalpensionstatistics.htm

Ruggie J. (2011). The UN protect, respect, remedy framework. Retrieved from https://media.business-humanrights.org/media/documents/files/reports-and-materials/Ruggie-protect-respect-remedy-framework.pdf

SwissOX. (2021). Swiss social stock exchange, the first liquid, regulated global impact investing market. Retrieved from https://www.sfgeneva.org/swisox-en/

Simone, C., et al. (2019). ((Intervento presentato al convegno New Challenges in Corporate Governance: Theory and Practice tenutosi a Napoli. Can the viable systems approach represent a lens to interpret barriers and enablers to the integration of sustainability? Evidence from an empirical experience. pp. 43–46.

United Nations. (2017). The 17 goals. Retrieved June 17, 2021, from https://sdgs.un.org/goals

Warde, C. P. (2018). The path to sustainability. Retrieved from https://www.cambridge.org/core/books/invention-of-sustainability/paths-to-sustained-growth-c-16501760/2E2C66D58314959F2FE2908DC5B1B8ED

Social Stock Exchanges

Adhana, D. (2020). Social stock exchange: An innovative financing platform for social Enterprises in India. *SSRN Electronic Journal*. https://doi.org/10.2139/ssrn.3619235

Agapitova, N., Sanchez, B., & Tinsley, E. (2017). *Government support to the social Enterprise sector: Comparative review of policy frameworks and tools*. World Bank Group. Retrieved from https://www.innovationpolicyplatform.org/www.innovationpolicyplatform.org/system/files/SE%20Policy%20Note_Jun20/in.dex.pdf

Bandini, C. (2014). Social stock exchanges—innovative financing for international development. *Social Justice, 7*, 24.

Battilana, J., & Lee, M. (2014). Advancing research on hybrid organizing – Insights from the study of social enterprises. *Academy of Management Annals, 8*(1), 397–441. https://doi.org/10.5465/19416520.2014.893615

Belleflamme, P., Lambert, T., & Schwienbacher, A. (2014). Crowdfunding: Tapping the right crowd. *Journal of Business Venturing, 29*(5), 585–609. https://doi.org/10.1016/j.jbusvent.2013.07.003

Bernardino, S., Santos, J., & Ribeiro, J. (2016). Social crowdfunding: A new model for financing regional development ? *Journal of Urban and Regional Analysis, 8*, 97–115.

Bernardino, S., & Freitas Santos, J. (2016). Financing social ventures by crowdfunding: The influence of entrepreneurs' personality traits. *The International Journal of Entrepreneurship and Innovation, 17*(3), 173–183.

Biancone, P. P., Secinaro, S., Brescia, V., & Calandra, D. (2019). Data quality methods and applications in health Care system: A systematic literature review. *International Journal of Business and Management, 14*(4), 35. https://doi.org/10.5539/ijbm.v14n4p35

Biancone, P., Secinaro, S., Brescia, V., & Iannaci, D. (2020). Business model innovation for sustainability and social impact. *International Journal of Management Sciences and Business Research, 9*(5), 30–40.

Boguslavskaya, S., & Demushkina, I. (2013). *Social stock exchange a new socio-economic phenomenon*. RIUESS.

Bugg-Levine, A., Kogut, B., & Kulatilaka, N. (2012, gennaio 1). A New Approach to Funding Social Enterprises. Harvard Business Review, January February 2012. https://hbr.org/2012/01/a-new-approach-to-funding-social-enterprises

Calderini, M., Chiodo, V., & Michelucci, F. V. (2018). The social impact investment race: Toward an interpretative framework. *European Business Review, 30*(1), 66–81. https://doi.org/10.1108/EBR-10-2016-0134

Chaturvedi, S., Sabyasachi, S., & Arun S., N. (2019). Social Stock Exchange for Social Enterprises and Social Incubators: An Exploratory Study for India | Research and Information System For Developing Countries. Research and Information System for Developing Countries. https://www.ris.org.in/social-stock-exchange-social-enterprises-and-social-incubators-exploratory-study-india

Colasanti, N., Frondizi, R., & Meneguzzo, M. (2020). Creating virtuous circles: Worker-managed firms and local communities. *Piccola Impresa / Small Business, 0*(2) Article 2. https://doi.org/10.14596/pisb.362

Dadush, S. (2015a). Regulating Social Finance: Can Social Stock Exchanges Meet the Challenge? (SSRN Scholarly Paper ID 2574921). Social Science Research Network. https://papers.ssrn.com/abstract=2574921

Dal Mas, F., Massaro, M., Lombardi, R., & Garlatti, A. (2019). From output to outcome measures in the public sector: A structured literature review. *International Journal of Organizational Analysis, 27*(5), 1631–1656. https://doi.org/10.1108/IJOA-09-2018-1523

Dart, R. (2004). The legitimacy of social enterprise. *Nonprofit Management and Leadership, 14*(4), 411–424. https://doi.org/10.1002/nml.43

Dees, J. G. (2018). The meaning of social entrepreneurship 1, 2. In J. Hamschmidt & M. Pirson (Eds.), *Case studies in social entrepreneurship and sustainability* (1st ed., pp. 22–30). Routledge. https://doi.org/10.4324/9781351278560-5

Doherty, B., Haugh, H., & Lyon, F. (2014). Social enterprises as hybrid organisations: A review and research agenda. *International Journal of Management Reviews, 16*(4), 417–436.

Elo, S., & Kyngäs, H. (2008). The qualitative content analysis process. *Journal of Advanced Nursing, 62*(1), 107–115. https://doi.org/10.1111/j.1365-2648.2007.04569.x

Falagas, M. E., Pitsouni, E. I., Malietzis, G. A., & Pappas, G. (2007). Comparison of PubMed, Scopus, web of science, and Google scholar: Strengths and weaknesses. *The FASEB Journal, 22*(2), 338–342. https://doi.org/10.1096/fj.07-9492LSF

Flick, U., von Kardoff, E., & Steinke, I. (2004). *A companion to qualitative research.* Sage.

Galaskiewicz, J., & Barringer, S. N. (2012). Social enterprises and social categories. In B. Gidron & Y. Hasenfeld (Eds.), *Social enterprises: An Organisational perspective* (pp. 47–70). Palgrave Macmillan. https://doi.org/10.1057/9781137035301_3

Galina, S., Rebehy, P., Carvalho, L., & Costa, M. (2013a). Determinants of attractiveness in social stock exchange. *Journal of Management and Sustainability, 3*, 157. https://doi.org/10.5539/jms.v3n4p157

Lecy, J. D., & Beatty, K. E. (2012). Representative literature reviews using constrained snowball sampling and citation Network analysis (SSRN scholarly paper ID 1992601). *Social Science Research Network.* https://doi.org/10.2139/ssrn.1992601

Liberati, A., Altman, D. G., Tetzlaff, J., Mulrow, C., Gøtzsche, P. C., Ioannidis, J. P. A., Clarke, M., Devereaux, P. J., Kleijnen, J., & Moher, D. (2009). The PRISMA statement for reporting systematic reviews and meta-analyses of studies that evaluate health Care interventions: Explanation and elaboration. *PLoS Medicine, 6*(7), e1000100. https://doi.org/10.1371/journal.pmed.1000100

Mair, J. (2010). Social Entrepreneurship: Taking Stock and Looking Ahead. Working Paper No. WP-888, 1–13. https://doi.org/10.2139/ssrn.1729642.

Massaro, M., Dumay, J., & Guthrie, J. (2016). On the shoulders of giants: Undertaking a structured literature review in accounting. *Accounting Auditing & Accountability Journal, 29*(5), 767–801. https://doi.org/10.1108/AAAJ-01-2015-193

Massaro, M., Dumay, J., Garlatti, A., & Dal Mas, F. (2018). Practitioners' views on intellectual capital and sustainability: From a performance-based to a worth-based perspective. *Journal of Intellectual Capital, 19*(2), 367–386. https://doi.org/10.1108/JIC-02-2017-0033

Mauksch, S., Dey, P., Rowe, M., & Teasdale, S. (2017). Ethnographies of social enterprise. *Social Enterprise Journal, 13*(02), 114–127. https://doi.org/10.1108/SEJ-03-2017-0019

McWade, W. (2012). The role for social enterprises and social Investors in the Development Struggle. *Journal of Social Entrepreneurship, 3*(1), 96–112. https://doi.org/10.1080/19420676.2012.663783

Meeks, K. (2018). Ulrichsweb Review. *Journal of Electronic Resources in Medical Libraries, 15*(1), 26–35. https://doi.org/10.1080/15424065.2018.1432436

Mendell, M., & Nogales, R. (2009). Social Enterprises in OECD Member Countries: What are the Financial Streams? 89–138. https://doi.org/10.1787/9789264055513-4-en.

Mongeon, P., & Paul-Hus, A. (2016). The journal coverage of web of science and Scopus: A comparative analysis. *Scientometrics, 106*(1), 213–228.

Moritz, A., & Block, J. H. (2016). Crowdfunding: A literature review and research directions. In D. Brüntje & O. Gajda (Eds.), *Crowdfunding in Europe: State of the art in theory and practice* (pp. 25–53). Springer International Publishing. https://doi.org/10.1007/978-3-319-18017-5_3

Paul, J., & Criado, A. R. (2020). The art of writing literature review: What do we know and what do we need to know? *International Business Review, 29*(4), 101717. https://doi.org/10.1016/j.ibusrev.2020.101717

Pavlov, R. (2017). Social stock exchange as a factor of increasing the innovation potential of social enterprises. In *ECIE 2017 12th European Conference on Innovation and Entrepreneurship.*

Pavlov, R. (2019). Determining the factors which deter the development of social entrepreneurship in Russia. In *European conference on innovation and entrepreneurship*. https://doi.org/10.34190/ECIE.19.096

Romme, A. G. L., Avenier, M.-J., Denyer, D., Hodgkinson, G. P., Pandza, K., Starkey, K., & Worren, N. (2015). Towards common ground and trading zones in management research and practice. *British Journal of Management, 26*(3), 544–559. https://doi.org/10.1111/1467-8551.12110

Secinaro, S., Corvo, L., Brescia, V., & Iannaci, D. (2019). Hybrid organisations: A systematic review of the current literature. *International Business Research, 12*(11), 1. https://doi.org/10.5539/ibr.v12n11p1

Smith, W., Gonin, M., & Besharov, M. (2013). Managing social-business tensions: A review and research agenda for social Enterprise. *Business Ethics Quarterly, 23*(3), 407–442.

Sparkes, R. (2001). Ethical investment: Whose ethics, which investment? *Business Ethics: A European Review, 10*(3), 194–205. https://doi.org/10.1111/1467-8608.00233

Steiner, A. (2016). The playground of the rich? Growing social business in the 21st century. *Social Enterprise Journal, 12*. https://doi.org/10.1108/SEJ-12-2015-0036

Wendt, K. (2017). Social stock exchanges—Democratisation of capital investing for impact. *SSRN Electronic Journal.* https://doi.org/10.2139/ssrn.3021739

Impact Investing

Arvidson, M., & Lyon, F. (2014). Social impact measurement and non-profit Organisations: Compliance, resistance, and promotion. *Voluntas: International Journal of Voluntary and Nonprofit Organizations, 25*(4), 869–886. https://doi.org/10.1007/s11266-013-9373-6

Bugg-Levine, A., & Emerson, J. (2011a). *Impact investing: Transforming how we make money while making a difference* (1st ed.). Jossey-Bass.

Bull, M. (2007). "Balance": The development of a social enterprise business performance analysis tool. *Social Enterprise Journal, 3*(1), 49–66. https://doi.org/10.1108/17508610780000721

Burdge, R. J., & Vanclay, F. (1996). Social impact assessment: A contribution to the state of the art series. *Impact Assessment, 14*(1), 59–86. https://doi.org/10.1080/07349165.1996.9725886

Brandstetter, L., & Lehner, O. M. (2014). *Impact investment portfolios: Including social risks and returns*. ACRN Oxford Publishing House. SSRN: http://ssrn.com/abstract=2519671

Brandstetter, L., & Lehner, O. M. (2015). Opening the market for impact investments: The need for adapted portfolio tools. *Entrepreneurship Research Journal, 5*(2), 87–107.

Carter, P., et al. (2018). The elusive quest for additionality. Retrieved from https://www.cgdev.org/sites/default/files/elusive-quest-additionality.pdf

Chiappini, H. (2017). *Social impact funds: Definition, assessment and performance*. Springer International Publishing.

Clark, C., Rosenzweig, W., Long, D., & Olsen, S. (2004). *Double bottom line project report: Assessing social impact in double bottom line ventures: Methods catalog*. ABT Associates. Retrieved from https://escholarship.org/uc/item/80n4f1mf

Corporation, I. F. (2019). Investing for impact: Operating principles for impact management. Retrieved from https://www.ifc.org/wps/wcm/connect/Topics_Ext_Content/IFC_External_Corporate_Site/Impact-investing/Principles/

Costa, E., & Pesci, C. (2016). Social impact measurement: Why do stakeholders matter? *Sustainability Accounting, Management and Policy Journal, 7*(1), 99–124. https://doi.org/10.1108/SAMPJ-12-2014-0092

Darby, L., & Jenkins, H. (2006). Applying sustainability indicators to the social enterprise business model: The development and application of an indicator set for Newport Wastesavers, Wales. *International Journal of Social Economics, 33*(5/6), 411–431. https://doi.org/10.1108/03068290610660689

Dufour, B. (2019). Social impact measurement: What can impact investment practices and the policy evaluation paradigm learn from each other? *Research in International Business and Finance, 47*, 18–30. https://doi.org/10.1016/j.ribaf.2018.02.003

Ebrahim, A., Battilana, J., & Mair, J. (2014). The governance of social enterprises: Mission drift and accountability challenges in hybrid organizations. *Research in Organizational Behavior, 34*, 81–100. https://doi.org/10.1016/j.riob.2014.09.001

Ebrahim, A., & Rangan, V. K. (2010). Putting the brakes on impact: A contingency framework for measuring social performance. *Academy of Management Proceedings, 2010*(1), 1–6. https://doi.org/10.5465/ambpp.2010.54500944

Ebrahim, A., & Rangan, V. K. (2014). What impact? *California Management Review, 56*(3), 118–141. https://doi.org/10.1525/cmr.2014.56.3.118

Emerson, J., Wachowicz, J., & Chun, S. (2000). Social return on investment: Exploring aspects of value creation in the nonprofit sector. *The Box Set: Social Purpose Enterprises Venture Philanthropy in the New Millennium., 2*, 130–173.

Freudenburg, W. R. (1986). Social impact assessment. *Annual Review of Sociology, 12*, 451–478.

Gentile, M. (2000). Social impact management: A definition. In *The Aspen Institute business and society program discussion paper II*. Retrieved from https://assets.aspeninstitute.org/content/uploads/files/content/docs/bsp/SOCIALIMPACTMANAGEMENT.PDF

Gibbon, J., & Dey, C. (2011). Developments in social impact measurement in the third sector: Scaling up or dumbing down? *Social and Environmental Accountability Journal, 31*(1), 63–72. https://doi.org/10.1080/0969160X.2011.556399

Gray, R. (2010). Is accounting for sustainability actually accounting for sustainability. . .and how would we know? An exploration of narratives of organisations and the planet. *Accounting, Organizations and Society, 35*(1), 47–62. https://doi.org/10.1016/j.aos.2009.04.006

Grieco, C. (2015). *Assessing social impact of social enterprises: Does one size really fit all?* Springer International Publishing.

Haski-Leventhal, D., & Mehra, A. (2016). Impact measurement in social enterprises: Australia and India. *Social Enterprise Journal, 12*(1), 78–103. https://doi.org/10.1108/SEJ-05-2015-0012

Hatry, H. P. (2013). Sorting the relationships among performance measurement, program evaluation, and performance management. *New Directions for Evaluation, 2013*(137), 19–32. https://doi.org/10.1002/ev.20043

Hoffman, S. A., & Olazabal, V. M. (2018). The next frontier for measurement and evaluation: Social impact measurement for impact investing and market solutions. *African Evaluation Journal, 6*(2), e1–e3. https://doi.org/10.4102/aej.v6i2.342

Hoskin, K. (1996). The "awful idea of accountability": Inscribing people into the measurement of objects. In R. Munro & J. Mouritsen (Eds.), *Accountability: Power, ethos and the Technologies of Managing London*. International Thomson Business Press.

Hubers, F. (2017). Assessing the Impact of Social Enterprises: An Exploration of the Methods and Criteria used by Impact Investors and Philanthropists in Asia (ACSEP: Social Entrepreneurship in Asia Working Paper No. 6). Retrieved from https://bschool.nus.edu.sg/acsep/wp-content/uploads/sites/19/2018/10/SWP6.pdf

Jackson, E. T., & Harji, K. (2012). *Unlocking capital, activating a movement: Final report of the strategic assessment of the rockefeller foundation's impact investing initiative*. The Rockefeller Foundation.

Jackson. (2013). Interrogating the theory of change: Evaluating impact investing where it matters most. *Journal of Sustainable Finance & Investment, 3*(2), 95–110. https://doi.org/10.1080/20430795.2013.776257

Lall, S. A. (2017). Measuring to improve versus measuring to prove: Understanding the adoption of social performance measurement practices in nascent social enterprises. *Voluntas: International Journal of Voluntary and Nonprofit Organizations, 28*(6), 2633–2657. https://doi.org/10.1007/s11266-017-9898-1

Lall, S. A. (2019). From legitimacy to learning: How impact measurement perceptions and practices evolve in social Enterprise–social finance organization relationships. *Voluntas: International Journal of Voluntary and Nonprofit Organizations*, 1–16. https://doi.org/10.1007/s11266-018-00081-5

Lam, S. S., & Tan, X. R. A. (2021). Towards a unifying framework of impact assessment in impact investing. In K. Wendt (Ed.), *Theories of change: Change leadership tools, models and applications for investing in sustainable development 2021*. Springer International Publishing.

Lam, S.-S., Zhang, W., & Jacob, G. H. (2015). The mispricing of socially ambiguous grey stocks. *Finance Research Letters, 13*, 81–89. https://doi.org/10.1016/j.frl.2015.02.010

Latané, B. (1981). The psychology of social impact. *American Psychologist, 36*(4), 343–356. https://doi.org/10.1037/0003-066X.36.4.343

Liket, K. C., Rey-Garcia, M., & Maas, K. E. H. (2014). Why Aren't evaluations working and what to do about it: A framework for negotiating meaningful evaluation in nonprofits. *American Journal of Evaluation, 35*(2), 171–188. https://doi.org/10.1177/1098214013517736

Louch, W., Ballard, E., & Clark, S. (2018). Abraaj investors hire auditor to trace money. *The Wall Street Journal*. Retrieved from https://www.wsj.com/articles/abraaj-investors-hire-auditor-to-trace-money-1517598630

Luke, B., Barraket, J., & Eversole, R. (2013). Measurement as legitimacy versus legitimacy of measures: Performance evaluation of social enterprise. *Qualitative Research in Accounting & Management, 10*(3/4), 234–258. https://doi.org/10.1108/QRAM-08-2012-0034

Maas, K., & Grieco, C. (2017). Distinguishing game changers from boastful charlatans: Which social enterprises measure their impact? *Journal of Social Entrepreneurship, 8*(1), 110–128. https://doi.org/10.1080/19420676.2017.1304435

Maas, K., & Liket, K. (2011). Social impact measurement: Classification of methods. In *Environmental management accounting and supply chain management* (pp. 171–202). Springer.

Meyer, J. W., & Rowan, B. (1977). Institutionalized organizations: Formal structure as myth and ceremony. *American Journal of Sociology, 83*(2), 340–363.

Molecke, G., & Pinkse, J. (2017). Accountability for social impact: A bricolage perspective on impact measurement in social enterprises. *Journal of Business Venturing, 32*(5), 550–568. https://doi.org/10.1016/j.jbusvent.2017.05.003

Mook, L., Maiorano, J., Ryan, S., Armstrong, A., & Quarter, J. (2015). Turning social return on investment on its head. *Nonprofit Management and Leadership, 26*(2), 229–246. https://doi.org/10.1002/nml.21184

Morgan, G. G. (2013). Purposes, activities and beneficiaries: Assessing the use of accounting narratives as indicators of third sector performance. *Qualitative Research in Accounting & Management, 10*(3/4), 295–315. https://doi.org/10.1108/QRAM-04-2013-0016

Mudaliar, A., Bass, R., & Dithrich, H. (2018). Annual impact investor survey. Retrieved from https://thegiin.org/research/publication/annualsurvey2018

Mudaliar, A., Bass, R., Dithrich, H., & Nova, N. (2019). *Annual impact investor survey*. Global Impact Investing Network (GIIN). Retrieved from https://thegiin.org/assets/GIIN_2019%20Annual%20Impact%20Investor%20Survey_webfile.pdf

Mudaliar, A., & Dithrich, H. (2019). Sizing the impact investing market. Retrieved from https://thegiin.org/assets/Sizing%20the%20Impact%20Investing%20Market_webfile.pdf

Mudaliar, A., Schiff, H., & Bass, R. (2016). Annual impact investor survey. Retrieved from https://thegiin.org/knowledge/publication/annualsurvey2016

Mudaliar, A., Pineiro, A., Bass, R., & Dithrich, H. (2017a). The state of impact measurement and management practice. Retrieved from https://thegiin.org/research/publication/imm-survey

Mudaliar, A., Schiff, H., Bass, R., & Dithrich, H. (2017b). Annual impact investor survey. *Retrieved from*. https://thegiin.org/research/publication/annualsurvey2017

Nations, U. (2019). We can end poverty: millennium development goals and beyond 2015. Retrieved from https://www.un.org/millenniumgoals/

Network, G. I. I. (2019a). About the GIIN. Retrieved from https://thegiin.org/about/.

Network, G. I. I. (2019b). Core characteristics of impact investing. Retrieved from https://thegiin.org/characteristics.

Network, G. I. I. (2019c). Iris+. Retrieved from https://iris.thegiin.org/.

Network, G. I. I. (2019d). IRIS+ and the five dimensions of impact. https://iris.thegiin.org/document/iris-and-the-five-dimensions/

Network, G. I. I. (2019e). Research. Retrieved from https://thegiin.org/research

Network, G. I. I. (2019f). What is impact investing? Retrieved from https://thegiin.org/impact-investing/need-to-know/#what-is-impact-investing

Nicholls, A. (2018). A general theory of social impact accounting: Materiality, uncertainty and empowerment. *Journal of Social Entrepreneurship, 9*(2), 132–153. https://doi.org/10.1080/19420676.2018.1452785

Nicholls, A., Paton, R., & Emerson, J. (2015). *Social finance* (1st ed.). Oxford University Press.

Ormiston, J., & Seymour, R. (2011). Understanding value creation in social entrepreneurship: The importance of aligning mission, strategy and impact measurement. *Journal of Social Entrepreneurship, 2*(2), 125–150. https://doi.org/10.1080/19420676.2011.606331

Owen, F., Li, J., Whittingham, L., Hope, J., Bishop, C., Readhead, A., & Mook, L. (2015). Social return on investment of an innovative employment option for persons with developmental disabilities. *Nonprofit Management and Leadership, 26*(2), 209–228. https://doi.org/10.1002/nml.21187

Paton, R. (2003). *Managing and measuring social enterprises*. SAGE.

Primack, D. (2018). Private equity firm Abraaj Capital is in turmoil. Retrieved from https://www.axios.com/the-1522167159-8ebfe0cb-7dcd-4385-8a00-27cf68cd39f2.html

Rawhouser, H., Cummings, M., & Newbert, S. L. (2019). Social impact measurement: Current approaches and future directions for social entrepreneurship research. *Entrepreneurship Theory and Practice, 43*(1), 82–115. https://doi.org/10.1177/1042258717727718

Ruff, K., & Olsen, S. (2018). The need for analysts in social impact measurement: How evaluators can help. *American Journal of Evaluation, 39*(3), 402–407. https://doi.org/10.1177/1098214018778809

Salazar, J., Husted, B. W., & Biehl, M. (2012). Thoughts on the evaluation of corporate social performance through projects. *Journal of Business Ethics, 105*(2), 175–186. https://doi.org/10.1007/s10551-011-0957-z

Schaltegger, S., & Burritt, R. (2018). Business cases and corporate engagement with sustainability: Differentiating ethical motivations. *Journal of Business Ethics, 147*(2), 241–259. https://doi.org/10.1007/s10551-015-2938-0

Spiess-Knafl, W., & Scheck, B. (2017). *Impact investing: Instruments, mechanisms and actors*. Springer International Publishing.

Taskforce, S. I. I. (2014). Measuring impact: Subject paper of the impact measurement working group. Retrieved from https://gsgii.org/reports/measuring-impact/

Weber, O. (2016a). Impact investing. In O. M. Lehner (Ed.), *Routledge handbook of social and sustainable finance*. Routledge.

Weber, O., & Feltmate, B. (2016a). *Sustainable banking: Managing the social and environmental impact of financial institutions*. University of Toronto Press.

Internet Sources

Global Impact Investing Rating System (GIIRS). (2012). *GIIRS quarterly analytics report: Q1 2012*. Global Impact Investing Rating System.

Stock Exchanges

Michie, R. (1987). *The London and New York stock exchanges 1850–1914 (Routledge revivals)*. Routledge.

NASDAQ: Glossary of financial terms. https://www.nasdaq.com/glossary/l/liquidity

Osterhelweg, O., & Schiereck, D. (1993). *Messkonzepte für die Liquidität von Finanzmärkten*. Manuskripte aus den Instituten für Betriebswirtschaftslehre der Universität Kiel. Retrieved from https://www.econstor.eu/bitstream/10419/149816/1/manuskript_308.pdf

Taxonomies

Bank Negara Malaysia. (2021). Climate change and principles based taxonomy. Retrieved from https://www.bnm.gov.my/-/climate-change-principle-based-taxonomy

China National Development and Reform Commission. (2019). Retrieved from https://www.ndrc.gov.cn/xxgk/zcfb/tz/201601/t20160108_963561.html

EU Action Plan. (2019). EU action plan for financing sustainable growth. Retrieved from https://eur-lex.europa.eu/legal-content/EN/TXT/?uri=CELEX:52018DC0097

EU Taxonomy. (2020). Retrieved from https://ec.europa.eu/info/business-economy-euro/banking-and-finance/sustainable-finance/eu-taxonomy-sustainable-activities_en

EU Strategy for Financing the Transition to a Sustainable Economy. Retrieved from https://ec.europa.eu/info/topics/banking-and-finance_en

EU Delegated Act. (2021). Retrieved from https://ec.europa.eu/finance/docs/level-2-measures/taxonomy-regulation-delegated-act-2021-2800_en.pdf

EU Delegated Act Annex 1. (2021). Retrieved from https://ec.europa.eu/finance/docs/level-2-measures/taxonomy-regulation-delegated-act-2021-2800-annex-1_en.pdf

EU Delegated Act Annex 2. (2021). Retrieved from https://ec.europa.eu/finance/docs/level-2-measures/taxonomy-regulation-delegated-act-2021-2800-annex-2_en.pdf

EU International Platform on Sustainable. (2021). Finance. Retrieved from https://ec.europa.eu/info/business-economy-euro/banking-and-finance/sustainable-finance/international-platform-sustainable-finance_en#members

ICMA. (2021). Overview and recommendation for sustainable finance taxonomies. Retrieved from https://www.icmagroup.org/assets/documents/Sustainable-finance/ICMA-Overview-and-Recommendations-for-Sustainable-Finance-Taxonomies-May-2021-180521.pdf?utm_source=ICMA+Total+Subscribes&utm_campaign=60d330c67f-EMAIL_CAMPAIGN_2_23_2021_18_40_COPY_02&utm_medium=email&utm_term=0_74a993020a-60d330c67f-75768878

Morningstar. (2021). EU action plan policy updates. Retrieved from https://www.investmentofficer.lu/en/partners/morningstar/morningstar-eu-action-plan-policy-updates-what-expect

Sustainalytics. (2021). Sustainable finance action plan. Retrieved from https://www.sustainalytics.com/investor-solutions/esg-research/eu-sustainable-finance-action-plan-solutions

Rogers et al (2018). In this sense impact investment uses the tools form development finance like integrating a programme theory often referred to as theory of change into the investment process. Rogers et al (2018) consider Programme theory or theory of change have two essential components, one conceptual and one empirical.They consist of an explicit theory or model of how the program causes the intended or observed outcomes and an evaluation that is guided by this model.

Blueprinting SSEs

Abraham, R. K. (2013). *Social stock exchange: A market oriented technology based solution for impact investment and transparency in social welfare projects*. Centre for Public Policy Research. Retrieved from http://www.cppr.in/article/social-stock-exchange-a-market-oriented-technology-based-solution-for-impact-investment-and-transparency-in-social-welfare-projects/

Addis, R. (2015). The role of government and policy in social finance. In A. Nicholls, R. Paton, & J. Emerson (Eds.), *Social finance* (pp. 383–459). Oxford University Press.

Aggrawal, R. (2002). Demutualization and corporate governance of stock exchanges. *Journal of Applied Corporate Governance, 15*(1), 105–113.

Aggrawal, R., & Dahiya, S. (2006). Demutualization and public offerings of financial exchanges. *Journal of Applied Corporate Finance, 18*(3), 96–106.

All Street Research. (2017). *Social stock exchange: Annual research book 2017*. All Street Research. Retrieved from http://socialstockexchange.com/wp-content/uploads/2017/02/SSX-Investor-Research-Book-2017-Final.pdf

Alliance. (2009). *GSIX - a global network for social investment*. Alliance Magazine. Retrieved from http://www.alliancemagazine.org/news/gsix-a-global-network-for-social-investment/

Alliance. (2010). *Social investment exchange to launch in Kenya*. Alliance Magazine. Retrieved from http://www.alliancemagazine.org/news/social-investment-exchange-to-launch-in-kenya/

Alois, J. (2014). *Mission markets offers up impact investing platform as catalyst for positive change*. Crowdfund Insider. Retrieved from https://www.crowdfundinsider.com/2014/06/41164-mission-markets-offers-impact-investing-platform-catalyst-positive-change/

Alter, K., Shoemaker, P., Tuan, M., & Emerson, J. (2001). *When is it time to say goodbye? Exit strategies and venture philanthropy funds*. Virtue Ventures, Social Venture Partners and The Roberts Foundation. Retrieved from http://www.virtueventures.com/files/exitstrategy.pdf

Barclays. (2017). *Compass: Q1 2017*. Barclays Wealth and Investment Management. Retrieved from https://wealth.barclays.com/content/dam/bwpublic/global/documents/BTH%20docs/Compass%20PDFs/compass-q1-2017.pdf

Baker, H. K., Singleton, J. C., & Veit, E. T. (2011). *Survey research in corporate finance: Bridging the gap between theory and practice*. Oxford University Press.

Barman, E. (2015). Of principle and principal: Value plurality in the market of impact investing. *Valuation Studies, 3*(1), 9–44.

Bernardino, S., & Santos, F. (2015). Financing social ventures by crowdfunding: The influence of entrepreneur's personality traits. Universidade do Minho NIPE Working Paper 12. Retrieved from http://www.nipe.eeg.uminho.pt/Uploads/WP_2015/NIPE_WP_12_2015.pdf

Bernardino, S., Santos, J. F., & Ribeiro, J. C. (2015). Social entrepreneurship: Does institutional environment make a difference? In L. Carvalho (Ed.), *Handbook of research on entrepreneurial success and its impact on regional development* (pp. 513–538). IGI Global.

Birkholz, C. (2015). Hybrid Organizing under Institutional Complexity: Insights from Impact Investing and Social Entrepreneurship. PhD Thesis. Univesity of St. Gallen. Retrieved from http://verdi.unisg.ch/www/edis.nsf/SysLkpByIdentifier/4394/$FILE/dis4394.pdf#page=69

Bishop, M., & Green, M. (2015). Philanthrocapitalism comes of age. In A. Nicholls, R. Paton, & J. Emerson, Social finance (pp. 113–132). Oxford University Press.

Bornstein, S. A. (2015). *Social stock exchanges*. Around Wall Street. Retrieved http://aroundwallstreet.com/2015/02/social-stock-exchanges/

BSA. (2006). *SA's social investment exchange*. Brand South Africa. Retrieved from https://www.brandsouthafrica.com/south-africa-fast-facts/social-facts/sasix

Bugg-Levine, A. (2016). *Impact investing - CPPP 2016 leadership forum: Panel discussion*. USC Price. Retrieved from https://www.youtube.com/watch?v=Gj3E9EAg2iI

Bugg-Levine, A., & Emerson, J. (2011b). *Impact investing: Transforming how we make money while making a difference*. Jossey-Bass.

Burand, D. (2015). Resolving impact investment disputes: When doing good goes bad. *Washington University Journal of Law & Policy, 48*, 55.

Butunyi, C. (2011). *Launch of social investment exchange set to raise activity*. The East African. Retrieved from http://www.theeastafrican.co.ke/business/2560-1175130-14ec6bu/index.html

Campanale, M. (2010). *Bring on the social stock exchange*. Alliance Magazine. Retrieved from http://www.alliancemagazine.org/analysis/bring-on-the-social-stock-exchange/

Care, R., & Wendt, K. (2018). Investing with impact: An integrated analysis between academics and practitioners. In M. La Torre & M. Calderini (Eds.), *ocial Impact Investing Beyond the SIB*. Springer International Publishing.

Certo, S. T., & Miller, T. (2008). Social entrepreneurship: Key issues and concepts. *Business Horizons, 51*(4), 267–271.

Chhichhia, B. (2014). Social stock exchanges - innovative financing for international development. *Social Justice, 7*. Retrieved from http://ecommons.luc.edu/social_justice/7/

Chhichhia, B. (2015). The rise of social stock exchanges. *Stanford Social Innovation Review.*. Retrieved from https://ssir.org/articles/entry/the_rise_of_social_stock_exchanges

Christopoulos, D., & Vogl, S. (2015). The motivation of social entrepreneurs: The roles, agendas and relations of altruistic economic actors. *Journal of Social Entrepreneurship, 6*, 1–30. https://doi.org/10.1080/19420676.2014.954254

Costa, T., & Carvalho, L. (2012). Portuguese social stock exchange - assessment of sustainability. In *Proceedings of the 7th European conference on innovation and entrepreneurship* (pp. 105–115). Polytechnic Institute of Santarém.

CSR. (2006). *The south African social investment exchange*. CSR-News. Retrieved from http://csr-news.net/main/2006/09/11/the-south- african-social-investment-exchange/

Dadush, S. (2015b). Regulating social finance: Can social stock exchanges meet the challenge? *University of Pennsylvania Journal of International Law, 37*(1), 139–230.

Daggers, J., & Nicholls, A. (2016). *The landscape of social impact investment research: Trends and opportunities*. Saïd Business School. Retrieved from http://www.sbs.ox.ac.uk/sites/default/files/research-projects/CRESSI/docs/the-landscape-of-social-impact- investment-research.pdf

Deloitte. (2016). *The Deloitte millennial survey 2016*. Deloitte Touche Tohmatsu Limited, Retrieved from. https://www2.deloitte.com/global/en/pages/about-deloitte/articles/gx-millennials-shifting-business-purpose.html

Dowling, E. (2017). In the wake of austerity: Social impact bonds and the Financialisation of the welfare state in Britain. *New Political Economy, 22*, 294–310.

Egan, D. (2011). *Time for a stock exchange with a real purpose*. The Guardian. Retrieved from https://www.theguardian.com/social-enterprise-network/2011/oct/19/time-stock-exchange-social-purpose

Elkington, J. (2004). Enter the triple bottom line. In A. Henriques & J. Richardson (Eds.), *The triple bottom line: Does it all add up?* (pp. 1–16). Routledge.

Ellis, K., Michaely, R., & O'Hara, M. (2000). When the underwriter is the market maker: An examination of trading in the IPO aftermarket. *The Journal of Finance, 55*(3), 1039–1074.

Emerson, J. (1996). Grants, debt and equity: The nonprofit capital market and its malcontents. In J. Emerson & F. Twersky (Eds.), *New social entrepreneurs: The success, challenge and lessons of non-profit Enterprise creation*. The Roberts Foundation.

Emerson, J. (2003). The blended value proposition: Integrating social and financial returns. *California Management Review, 45*(4), 35–51. Retrieved from http://www.blendedvalue.org/wp-content/uploads/2004/02/pdf-proposition.pdf

Emerson, J., & Wachowicz, J. (2000). Riding the bleeding edge: A framework for tracking equity in the social sector and the creation of a nonprofit stock market. In *REDF box set: Social purpose enterprises and venture philanthropy in the new millennium*. REDF. Retrieved from http://www.blendedvalue.org/wp-content/uploads/2015/10/Bleeding-Edge.pdf

Epstein, G. A. (2005). *Financialization and the world economy*. Edward Elgar Publishing.

Ethex. (2017). *The story behind Ethex*. Ethex. Retrieved from https://www.ethex.org.uk/the-story-behind-ethex_55.html

Fairlie, R. W., Morelix, A., Reedy, E., & Russell, J. (2015). *The Kauffman index: Startup activity*. Eqing Marion Kauffman Foundation. Retrieved from http://www.kauffman.org/kauffman-index/reporting/startup-activity

FASE. (2016). Achieving impact for impact investing: A roadmap for developed countries. In *Financing agency for social entrepreneurship*. Ashoka Germany, and McKinsey & Company. Retrieved from http://germany.ashoka.org/sites/germany.ashoka.org/files/FASE-Ashoka-McKinsey_2016_Report-Impact-Investment.pdf

Field, A. (2012). *New impact investing stock exchange is making steady Progress*. Forbes. Retrieved from https://www.forbes.com/sites/annefield/2012/08/30/new-impact-investing-stock-exchange-is-making-steady-progress/#2255c3df35bb

Floyd, D. (2013). *Social stock exchange - the rise of international competitors*. The Guardian. Retrieved from https://www.theguardian.com/social-enterprise-network/2013/oct/24/canadian-social-stock-exchange

Forbes. (2014). Retrieved November 20, 2019, from https://www.forbes.com/forbes/welcome/?toURL=//www.forbes.com/sites/ashoka/2014/03/27/stock-exchanges-for-social-enterprises-heres-where-you-can-find-them/&refURL=&referrer=#4f673e7a4e5a

Fury, B. (2010). *Social Enterprise development in South Africa - creating a virtuous circle*. Tshikululu Social Investments. Retrieved from http://www.tshikululu.org.za/uploads/files/TSI_research_social-enterprise_2010.pdf

Galina, S. V., Rebehy, P. C., Carvalho, L. M., & da Costa, M. T. (2013b). Determinants of attractiveness in social stock exchange. *Journal of Management and Sustainability, 3*(4), 157–172.

Germak, A. J., & Robinson, J. A. (2014). Exploring the motivation of nascent social entrepreneurs. *Journal of Social Entrepreneurship, 5*(1), 5–21.

GEXSI. (2017). *The vision: A global Network of social investment exchanges*. GEXSI - The Global Exchange for Social Investment. Retrieved from http://green-oils.com/gexsi_initiatives.htm

Global Impact Investing Network. (2011). Impact-based incentive structures. Retrieved from https://thegiin.org/knowledge/publication/impact-based-incentive-structures-aligning-fund-manager-compensation-with-soci

Global Impact Investing Network. (2013). Catalytic first-loss capital. Retrieved from https://thegiin.org/knowledge/publication/catalytic-first-loss-capital, https://iris.thegiin.org/metric/5.0/od6350/

Global Impact Investing Network GIIN. (2016a). *Annual impact investor survey*. Gobal impact investing network. Retrieved from https://thegiin.org/assets/2016%20GIIN%20Annual%20Impact%20Investor%20Survey_Web.pdf

Global Impact Investing Network GIIN. (2016b). *Impact investing trends: Evidence of a growing industry*. Global Impact Investing Network. Retrieved from https://thegiin.org/assets/GIIN_Impact%20InvestingTrends%20Report.pdf

Global Impact Investing Network GIIN. (2016c). Impact investing trends: Theory of change Retrieved from https://iris.thegiin.org/metric/5.0/od6350/

Global Impact Investing Network. (2017a). Achieving the sustainable development goals: The role of impact investing. Retrieved from https://thegiin.org/knowledge/publication/sdgs-impinv

Global Impact Investing Network. (2017b). Impact measurement in the health sector. Retrieved from https://thegiin.org/knowledge/publication/network-insights-impact-measurement-in-the-healthcare-sector

Global Impact Investing Network and Dalberg Global Development Advisors. (2015). The landscape for impact investing in South Asia. Retrieved from https://thegiin.org/knowledge/publication/the-landscape-for-impact-investing-in-south-asia

Glänzel, G., Krlev, G., Schmitz, B., & Mildenberger, G. (2013). Report on the Feasibility and Opportunities of Using Various Instruments for Capitalising Social Innovators. The Theoretical, Empirical and Policy Foundations for Building Social Innovation in Europe" (TEPSIE). Retrieved from http://www.tepsie.eu/images/documents/tepsie43final.pdf

Gödker, K., & Mertins, L. (2015). The Effects of CSR-related Information in Investment Decisions: A Behavioral Finance Perspective. Unpublished manuscript.

Grossman, A., Appleby, S., & Reimers, C. (2013). Venture philanthropy: Its evolution and its future. *Harvard Business Review.*. Retrieved from https://avpn.asia/wp-content/uploads/2013/07/VP_Its_Evolution_and_Its_Future_6_13_13_copy.pdf

Hartigan, P. (2006). Delivering on the promise of social entrepreneurship: Challenges faced in launching a global social capital market. In A. Nicholls (Ed.), *Social entrepreneurship: New models of sustainable social change* (pp. 329–355). Oxford University Press.

Hartzell, J. (2007). *Creating an ethical stock exchange*. Saïd Business School, Oxford University. Retrieved from http://www.sbs.ox.ac.uk/sites/default/files/Skoll_Centre/Docs/Ethical%20stock%20exchange.pdf

Heinecke, A., Achleitner, A.-K., Spiess-Knafl, W., Schöning, M., & Noble, A. (2011). *Social investment manual - an introduction for social entrepreneurs*. Schwab Foundation for Social Entrepreneurship; Technische Universität München. Retrieved from http://www3.weforum.org/docs/WEF_Social_Investment_Manual_Final.pdf

Hynes, B. (2009). Growing the social enterprise–issues and challenges. *Social Enterprise Journal, 5*(2), 114–125.

Höchstädter, A. K., & Scheck, B. (2015). What's in a name: An analysis of impact investing understandings by academics and practitioners. *Journal of Business Ethics, 132*(2), 449–475.

IIX. (2013). *Nexii and IIX: Integrating global efforts for greater impact*. Impact Investment Exchange Asia. Retrieved from http://iixglobal.com/2013/05/nexii-and-iix-integrating-global-efforts-for-greater-impact/

IIX. (2017). *Asian impact investing firm IIX unveils a new look and goes global*. PR Newswire. Retrieved from http://www.prnewswire.com/news-releases/asian-impact-investing-firm-iix-unveils-a-new-look-and-goes-global-300405628.html

Jacobs, M., & Mazzucato, M. (2016). *Rethinking capitalism: Economics and policy for sustainable and inclusive growth*. Wiley- Blackwell.

John, R., & Emerson, J. (2015). Venture philanthropy: Development, evolution, and scaling around the world. In A. Nicholls, R. Paton, & J. Emerson (Eds.), *Social finance* (pp. 185–206). Oxford University Press.

Kleissner, C. (2019). Introduction. In K. Wendt (Ed.), *Positive impact investing*. Springer.

Kramer, M. R., & Porter, M. E. (2011). Creating shared value. *Harvard Business Review, 89*(1/2), 62–77.

Lazonick, W., & Mazzucato, M. (2012). *The risk-reward nexus: Innovation*. Finance and Inclusive Growth. Policy Network. Retrieved from http://www.policy-network.net/publications/4295/The-Risk-Reward-Nexus

Leadbeater, C. (1997). *The rise of the social entrepreneur*. Demos.

Lee, P. M.-D. (2008). A review of the theories of corporate social responsibility: Its evolutionary path and the road ahead. *International Journal of Management Reviews, 10*(1), 53–73.

Lehner, O. M. (2016a). Preface. In O. M. Lehner (Ed.), *Routledge handbook of social and sustainable finance* (pp. xxxv–xl). Routledge.

Lehner, O. M. (2016b). *Routledge handbook of social and sustainable finance*. Routledge International Handbooks.

Lehner, O. M., & Nicholls, A. (2014). Social finance and crowdfunding for social enterprises: A public-private case study providing legitimacy and leverage. *An International Journal of Entrepreneurial Finance, 16*(3), 271–286.

Lehner, O. M., & Germak, A. J. (2014). Antecedents of social entrepreneurship: Between public service motivation and the need for achievement. *International Journal of Social Entrepreneurship and Innovation, 3*(3), 214–229.

Lélé, S. M. (1991). Sustainable development: A critical review. *World Development, 19*(6), 607–621.

Letts, C. W., Ryan, W. P., & Grossman, A. S. (1997). *Virtuous capital: What foundations can learn from venture capitalists*. Harvard Business Review. Retrieved from https://hbr.org/1997/03/virtuous-capital-what-foundations-can-learn-from-venture-capitalists

Mair, J., & Noboa, E. (2006). Social entrepreneurship: How intentions to create a social venture are formed. In *Social entrepreneurship* (pp. 121–135). Palgrave Macmillan.

Martin, M. (2016). *Building the impact economy*. Springer.

Mendell, M., & Barbosa, E. (2013). Impact investing: A preliminary analysis of emergent primary and secondary exchange platforms. *Journal of Sustainable Finance and Investment, 3*(2), 111–123.

Monitor Institute. (2009a). *Investing for social and environmental impact*. Monitor Institute. Retrieved from http://monitorinstitute.com/downloads/what-we-think/impact-investing/Impact_Investing.pdf

NEF. (2006). *Developing a social equity capital market 2006*. Charities Aid Foundation. Retrieved from http://b.3cdn.net/nefoundation/37dafe6e1077aefebc_fam6bk6l3.pdf

Newsweek. (2008). Brazil: a stock exchange for do-gooders. Newsweek. Retrieved from http://www.newsweek.com/brazil-stock-exchange-do-gooders-89521

Nicholls, A., & Patton, A. (2015). Projection, valuation and pricing in social finance. In I. A. Nicholls, R. Paton, & J. Emerson (Eds.), *Social Finance* (pp. 311–334). Oxford University Press.

Nicholls, A., & Pharoah, C. (2008). *The landscape of social investment: A holistic typology of opportunities and challenges*. Saïd Business School. Retrieved from http://www.sbs.ox.ac.uk/sites/default/files/Skoll_Centre/Docs/Landscape%20of%20Social%20Investment.pdf

O'Donohoe, N., Leijonhufvud, C., & Saltuk, Y. (2010). Impact investments. In *An emerging asset class*. J. P. Morgan and Global Impact Investing Network. Retrieved from https://thegiin.org/assets/documents/Impact%20Investments%20an%20Emerging%20Asset%20Class2.pdf

OECD. (2014). *New investment approaches for addressing social and economic challenges*. Organisation for Economic Co-operation and Development. Retrieved from http://www.oecd.org/officialdocuments/publicdisplaydocumentpdf/?cote=DSTI/IND(2013)15/FINAL&docLanguage=En

OECD. (2015). *Social impact investment. Building the evidence base*. Organisation for Economic Co-operation and Development. Retrieved from http://www.oecd.org/sti/ind/social-impact-investment.pdf

OECD. (2016). *Entrepreneurship at a glance 2016*. Organisation for Economic Co-operation and Development. Retrieved from http://www.oecd-ilibrary.org/industry-and-services/entrepreneurship-at-a-glance_22266941

Poon, D. (2011). *The emergence and development of social enterprise sectors*. University of Pennsylvania. Retrieved from http://repository.upenn.edu/cgi/viewcontent.cgi?article=1010&context=sire

Peredo, A. M., & McLean, M. (2006). Social entrepreneurship: A critical review of the concept. *Journal of World Business, 41*(1), 56–65.

Preda, A. (2005). The investor as a cultural figure of global capitalism. In K. K. Cetina & A. Preda (Eds.), *The sociology of financial markets* (pp. 141–162). Oxford University Press.

Redclift, M. (2005). Sustainable development (1987–2005): An oxymoron comes of age. *Sustainable Development, 13*(4), 212–227.

Rexhepi, G. (2016). The architecture of social finance. In O. M. Lehner (Ed.), *Routledge handbook of social and sustainable finance* (pp. 35–49). Routledge.

RGB. (2011). Welcome page. Retrieved from RGB Exchange. http://www.rgbexchange.org

Rizzello, A., Caré, R., Migliazza, M. C., & Trotta, A. (2016). Social impact investing: A model and research agenda. In O. Lehner (Ed.), *Routledge handbook of social and sustainable finance*. Routledge.

Ritchie, A., & Emes, A. (2014). *The social venture connexion: A Canadian model for impact investing*. Association of Corporate Counsel. Retrieved from http://www.acc.com/_cs_upload/vl/membersonly/ACCDocketArticle/1362980_1.pdf

Robinson, J. (2006). Navigating social and institutional barriers to markets: How social entrepreneurs identify and evaluate opportunities. In *Social entrepreneurship* (pp. 95–120). Palgrave Macmillan.

Sacchetti, S., & Campbell, C. (2014). Social enterprise networks and social capital: A case study in Scotland. In *Social capital and economics: Social values, power, and social identity* (pp. 215–235). Routledge.

Schwabel, D. (2017). *Millenials might not be as entrepreneurial as you think*. World Economic Forum. Retrieved from https://www.weforum.org/agenda/2017/02/millennials-arent-the-entrepreneurial-generation-you-might-think-they-are

Schmitz, J., & Schrader, J. (2013). Corporate social Responsbility: A microeconomic review of the literature. *Journal of Economic Reviews, 29*(1), 27–45.

Schwartz, R., Jones, C., & Nicholls, A. (2015). Building the social finance infrastructure. In A. Nicholls, R. Paton, & J. Emerson (Eds.), *Social finance* (pp. 488–520). Oxford University Press.

Shahnaz, D., Kraybill, R., & Salamon, L. M. (2014). Social and environmental exchanges. In L. M. Salamon (Ed.), *New Frontiers of philanthropy. A guide to new tools and actors reshaping global philanthropy and social investing* (pp. 144–164). Oxford University Press.

Shaw, E., & Carter, S. (2007). Social entrepreneurship: Theoretical antecedents and empirical analysis of entrepreneurial processes and outcomes. *Journal of Small Business and Enterprise Development, 14*(3), 418–434.

Shiller, R. J. (2013). *Finance and the good society*. Princeton University Press.

Socialab. (2013). Colombia's Social Stock Exchange. Retrieved from Socialab. http://comunidad.socialab.com/ideas/ver/15162

Sparkes, R., & Cowton, C. J. (2004). The maturing of socially responsible investment: A review of the developing link with corporate social responsibility. *Journal of Business Ethics, 52*(1), 45–57.

Spence, A. (2014). How SVX is Scaling Social Innovation Across Borders. Retrieved from MaRS Discovery District. https://www.marsdd.com/news-and-insights/svx-us-scaling-social-innovation/

Spence, A., & Sinopoli, T. (2013). SVX - Case Study. MaRS Discovery District. Retrieved from http://s3.amazonaws.com/svx.production/cms/files/files/000/000/007/MaRS_SVX_Case_Study-original.pdf

Stiftung, B. (2016). *Social impact investment in Germany: Market report 2016 - from momentum to implemenation*. BertelsmannStiftung. Retrieved from http://www.bertelsmann-stiftung.de/fileadmin/files/user_upload/Market_Report_SII_in_Germany_2016.pdf

Stanley, M. (2015). Sustainable signals: The individual investor perspective. Morgan Stanley Institute for Sustainable Investing. Retrieved from https://www.morganstanley.com/sustainableinvesting/pdf/Sustainable_Signals.pdf.

SVX. (2013). SVX - Investor Manual. MaRS Discovery District. Retrieved from http://s3.amazonaws.com/svx.production/cms/files/files/000/000/002/SVX_Investor_Manual-original.pdf

The Economist. (2006). *The birth of Philanthrocapitalism*. The Economist. Retrieved from http://www.economist.com/node/5517656

The Economist. (2017). *'Impact investing' inches from niche to mainstream*. The Economist. Retrieved from http://www.economist.com/news/finance-and-economics/21713839-more-and-more-investors-are-looking-beyond-just-financial-returns-impact-investing

Thompson, J., Alvy, G., & Lees, A. (2000). Social entrepreneurship–a new look at the people and the potential. *Management Decision, 38*(5), 328–338.

Thorpe, R., Holt, R., Macpherson, A., & Pittaway, L. (2005). Using knowledge within small and medium-sized firms: A systematic review of the evidence. *International Journal of Management Reviews, 7*(4), 257–281.

Thümler, E. (2016). Financialization of philanthropy. In T. Jung, S. D. Phillips, & J. Harrow (Eds.), *The Routledge companion to philanthropy* (pp. 362–374). Routledge.

Tranfield, D., Denyer, D., & Smart, P. (2003). Towards a methodology for developing evidence-informed management knowledge by means of systematic review. *British Journal of Management, 14*(3), 207–222.

Toniic. (2016). *T100: Launch - insights from the frontier of impact investing*. Toniic Institute. Retrieved from http://www.toniic.com/t100/insights-from-the-frontier-of-impact-investing/

UN. (2015). Transforming Our World: the 2030 Agenda for Sustainable Development. Retrieved from Sustainable Development Knowledge Platform. https://sustainabledevelopment.un.org/post2015/transformingourworld

UNFCCC. (2015). Adoption of the Paris Agreement. Retrieved from United Nations Framework Convention on Climate Change. https://unfccc.int/resource/docs/2015/cop21/eng/l09r01.pdf

Wallis, M., & Klein, C. (2015). Ethical requirement and financial interest: A literature review on socially responsible investing. *Business Research, 8*(1), 61–98.

Weber, O. (2013). Impact measurement in microfinance: Is the measurement of the social return on investment an innovation in microfinance? *Journal of Innovation Economics & Management, 11*, 149–171.

Weber, O. (2016b). Impact investing. In O. M. Lehner (Ed.), *Routledge handbook of social and sustainable finance*. Routledge.

Weber, O., & Feltmate, B. (2016b). *Sustainable banking: Managing the social and environmental impact of financial institutions*. University of Toronto Press.

Weed, M. (2005). "Meta interpretation": A method for the interpretive synthesis of qualitative research. In *Forum qualitative Sozialforschung/forum: Qualitative social research* (Vol. 6(4)).

The World Economic Forum WEF. (2013). Bringing impact investing from the margins to the mainstream. Available at https://thegiin.org/knowledge/publication/bringing-impact-investing-from-the-margins-to-the-mainstream

Wheeler, P. (2006). *Towards a social stock exchange - barking up the wrong tree?* Alliance Magazine. Retrieved from http://www.alliancemagazine.org/feature/towards-a-social-stock-exchange-barking-up-the-wrong-tree/

Wilson, K. E. (2014). New investment approaches for addressing social and economic challenges. In *OECD science, technology and industry policy papers, no. 15*. OECD Publishing. Retrieved from http://www.oecd-ilibrary.org/docserver/download/5jz2bz8g00jj- en.pdf

Zandee, D. (2004). *BOVESPA and the social stock exchange: Mobilizing the financial market for development*. Case Western Reserve University. Retrieved from http://icepoverty.pbworks.com/f/bovespa_cs.pdf

Zingales, L. (2015). *Does finance benefit society?* National Bureau of Economic Research.

Social Entrepreneurship

Adner. (2017). Ecosystem as structure: An actionable construct for strategy. *Journal of Management, 43*(1), 39–58.

Alter K. (2007). Social enterprise typology. Retrieved from www.4lenses.org/setypology/print

Austin, et al. (2006). Social and commercial entrepreneurship: Same, different, or both? *Entrepreneurship Theory and Practice, 30*(2006), 1–23.

Brown, M. S., & Metter, R. (Eds.). (2007). *Giving USA 2007: The annual report on philanthropy for the year 2006*. Giving USA Foundation.

CASE. (2003). Center for the Advancement of Social Entrepreneurship. Nonpro t geographic expansion: Branches, af liates, or both? Durham, NC, 2003. Retrieved from www.caseatduke.org/documents/workingpaper4.pdf

CASE – Center for the Advancement of Social Entrepreneurship. (2006). The CASE 2005 Scaling Social Impact Survey: A Summary of the Findings. Princeton. Retrieved from www.caseatduke.org/documents/scalingsocialimpact_nalreport.pdf

Cheng, P., Goodall, E., Hodgkinson, R., & Kingston, J. (2010). *Financing the big society: Why social investment matters*. Charities Aid Foundation Venturesome. Retrieved from www.cafonline.org

Chong P., & Kleemann L. (2004). The Future of Funding for Social Enterprises.

Moore, J. (1993). Predators and prey: A new ecology of competition. *Harvard Business Review, 71*, 75–86. https://hbr.org/1993/05/predators-and-prey-a-new-ecology-of-competition

Dees, et al. (2004). Scaling social impact: Strategies for spreading social innovations. *Stanford Social Innovation Review, 1*(4), 14–32.

Emerson, J., & Spitzer, J. (2007). From Fragmentation to Functionality: Critical Concepts and Writings on Social Capital Market Structure, Operation, and Innovation. In: *Skoll Center for Social Entrepreneurship*.

Kraussa, N., & Walter, I. (2008). Can microfinance reduce portfolio volatility? NYU Working Paper No. FIN-07-054. Retrieved from https://papers.ssrn.com/sol3/papers.cfm?abstract_id=1300784

Mintzberg. (1980/1989). The Nature of Managerial Work. Retrieved from https://www.researchgate.net/publication/44834661_The_Nature_of_Managerial_Work

Monitor Institute. (2009b). Investing for Social and Environmental Impact. Retrieved from http://www.monitorinstitute.com/impactinvesting/

Monitor Institute. (2008). Market-Based Solutions to Social Change in India, 2008. Monitor Inclusive Markets Study. Retrieved from www.mim.monitor.com

Nicholls, A., (2007). What is the future of social Enterprise in Ethical Markets?, London, office of the third sector. Retrieved from www.cabinetoffice.gov.uk/third_sector/Research_and_statistics/social_enterprise_research/think_piec es.aspx.

Nicholls, A. (2008). Capturing the performance of the socially entrepreneurial organisation (SEO): An Organisational legitimacy approach. In *Social entrepreneurship*. Palgrave Macmillan.

Rothschild, M. (1990). *Bionomics: Economy as business ecosystem*. Beard Books.

Stiftung, B. (Hrsg). (2015). Scaling Social Impact. Retrieved from https://www.bertelsmann-stiftung.de/fileadmin/files/user_upload/BST_ScalingSocialImpactInEurope_final.pdf

Stiftung, B. (Hrsg). Skalierung sozialer Wirkungen: Handbuch zur Strategie und Erfolgsfaktoren von Sozialunternehmen. Retrieved from https://www.bertelsmann-stiftung.de/de/publikationen/publikation/did/skalierung-sozialer-wirkung/

Von Krogh, G., & Cusumano, M. A. (2001). Three strategies for: Managing fast growth. *Sloan Management Review, 42*(2), 53.

Weber, et al. (2012). Scaling social enterprises – A theoretically grounded framework. In A. Zacharakis, C. Brush, G. Bruton, A. Corbett, D. Dimov, L. Edelman, M. Gruber, B. Honig, B. Leleux, S. Matusik, M. Schindehutte, J. Sohl, & R. Sørheim (Eds.), *Frontiers of entrepreneurship research* (pp. 752–766). Babson College.

Winter, S., & Szulanski, G. (2001). Replication as strategy. *Organization Science, 12*(2001), 730–743.

The manufacturer's authorised representative in the EU is Springer Nature Customer Service Centre GmbH, Europaplatz 3, 69115 Heidelberg, Germany. If you have any concerns regarding our products, please contact ProductSafety@springernature.com

Printed and bound by CPI Group (UK) Ltd, Croydon, CR0 4YY
30/09/2026
02225472-0014